the ULTIMATE GUIDE to 21ST-CENTURY DATING

the ULTIMATE GUIDE to 21ST-CENTURY DATING

CAROL DIX

First published in 2007 by Fusion Press,
a division of Satin Publications Ltd
101 Southwark Street
London SE1 0JF
UK
info@visionpaperbacks.co.uk
www.visionpaperbacks.co.uk
Publisher: Sheena Dewan

All statistics and figures used within this book were valid at the time of going to press but can change rapidly in the online world.

A catalogue record for this book is available from the British Library.

ISBN: 978-1-905745-11-1

2 4 6 8 10 9 7 5 3 1

Cover and text design by ok?design
Printed and bound in the UK by
Mackays of Chatham Ltd, Chatham, Kent

Contents

Acknowledgements

I would like to express my thanks to the people at Parship.co.uk for their enthusiastic help and support while I was writing this book, and especially to Dr Victoria Lukats, psychiatrist and Parship's relationship and dating expert, for giving me permission to use her quizzes. They are fun to work with and take their match-making seriously. Similarly, thanks to the *Guardian* Soulmates team for helping put me in touch with members who were happy to tell their stories. The Writers Guild and writers association '26' (www.26.org.uk) were kind enough to contact members with a request to be part of this book. And Mary Balfour of Drawing Down the Moon introduction agency was also gracious with her support. The Appendix is adapted slightly from material available online from AOL.

Most importantly, my thanks go to all those women and men who have shared their secrets with me, talked willingly about the ups and downs of dating, and with whom I've enjoyed many a long hour over a pizza and glass of wine. I could not have written the book without their involvement. They have all been given fictional names to protect their identities.

Thanks to Louise Coe at Fusion Press for being understanding and helpful during the writing process, and to Vanessa Holt, my agent, with whom I worked many years ago on other books that have charted the course of my own life – from pregnancy, to motherhood, to women's careers, and now to a look at the amazing changing world of relationships and dating.

As a journalist, and author of many books, I have found writing this to be one of the best challenges. The world around us changes so fast, as does the way we lead our lives, so that sometimes it feels impossible to keep up. My family and friends across the world have had to listen to me talking, or sharing emails, about the project for many long months. So thanks to them too for their loving support.

Introduction

You're going to an interview for a new job. You're nervous, slightly sweaty, but you've prepared yourself, read up about the company, honed your CV, made sure you're dressed reasonably to give a smart and hopefully good impression. You've prepared some questions to ask them. You walk in the room and know that all eyes are glaring not at you, but through to the other side. They're assessing their first impression of you. Are you slightly overweight, obviously tense and nervous? Are you young or old for your given age? Do you answer their questions clearly and with a voice that expresses optimism and enthusiasm? Or is your head down into your chest, shoulders hunched, legs twisted uncomfortably?

The only things they're not doing are:

- assessing whether they would like to go to bed with you;
- wondering whether they might fall in love with you;
- trying to figure whether you could be the one person they might like to marry, have children or spend the next 30 years with.

So how crazy is dating?

Yes, this is exactly what we do to each other. We put ourselves through the agony of a job interview, or audition as an actor, and topload it with some of the most seriously difficult demands on another person we could ever possibly impose. And if that person does not meet all those criteria, we say goodbye, never to see them again.

I say this by way of my introduction to this book, *The Ultimate Guide to 21st-Century Dating*, because, after extensive research and interviews with a range of interesting and wonderful men and women, I've come away very impressed that anyone ever actually meets 'the one'. But the really good news is that they do. And it usually is by chance. However, the main point to consider for anyone who magically and mysteriously finds themselves, out of the blue, with their man or woman of choice, is that they did not meet this person by shutting themselves away in a locked room and spending all their days, evenings or weekends on their own. They met this person either by actively looking, searching, exploring life, or using the various dating methods that exist today in the 21st century.

Dating today is very different from how it was at any other time in the past. Why? The most obvious change has been brought about by the rapid growth in internet usage and subsequent rise in new online dating sites. Whoever would have thought, even ten years ago, we'd soon be choosing our potential mates as we might sort out an online grocery shopping list? We search for houses, holidays, clothes, books, music, mortgages, loans, courses, cars and almost everything online. Now, looking for interesting people has become as normal and taken for granted as any other form of service we might be seeking.

Dating has become mainstream in western society because we need help in meeting people. We all know that old-fashioned ways of match-making or getting together have more or less vanished. Most of us work far too many hours and office romances tend to be frowned upon. There's a terrible isolation to modern life, especially in cities where we rush along busy streets, not looking others in the eye, and scuttle into our houses or flats like rabbits going into the hutch. Once school, university or college days are over, the easy free-for-all of getting to know a large group of people in a non-threatening way more or less vanishes. Yet the isolation doesn't mean we want to live on our own or go about our daily lives in a solitary fashion. The human need for companionship, friendship, love, romance and sexual harmony have certainly not diminished at all.

This book is not only about dating pursued via the internet. Look at all the varied forms and exciting new ways that dating entrepreneurs are inventing to help us break the isolation and bring us together. Old-style introduction agencies still exist and continue to thrive. Speed dating is another form of face-to-face get-together, which, by packing as many people into a room as possible, probably mirrors the old village dance/marriage market our ancestors used to enjoy.

With so many singles in modern society, whole new ways of meeting and matching are being invented as we live and breathe – singles nights in bars, dinner dating societies, or groups organised to enhance your social life as well as potential marital hopes. There are hobby-based groups, cultural exchanges, holidays for singles, dance dating, dinners in the dark. New ideas are being dreamed up as I write.

You're in good company

One thing you can be sure of is that you are in the company of millions of like-minded people. In the United Kingdom there are some 9 million eligible singles, and a good 6 million have used some sort of dating service. Of these singles, 3.5 million are registered on online dating sites – that seems an awful lot of choice! And in the United States, one of the largest internet sites, Match.com, claims to have more than 15 million members worldwide. Surely there must be someone suitable for you in that kind of number? But would you have the energy to meet them all?

And here we come to the nub of the modern dating game. What to one person might be the most amazing opportunity for getting out and meeting loads of potential new partners, to another can appear daunting, terrifying and exhausting. What I've done in this book is try to bring the story of dating home, to you the reader, just as I needed to for myself. I've injected humanity, real life stories and names into the statistics or jargon, so you will begin to feel more comfortable with the topic as a whole. Dating can be fun or scary, it can mean a lot of rejection and pain, yet it just might lead to new connections, an improved sex life or, who knows, meeting that special person.

Unlike many authors of similarly titled books, I know about all this because I've been through it myself. Having been married for ten years, with a great love of my life, and raised two charming (OK then, yes, and lovely) daughters, I found myself on my own in my mid-40s. Over the ensuing years, I've probably experienced most of the normal forms of dating. In the pre-internet days, I tried the personal ads in print newspapers and received handwritten letters (doesn't that sound quaint now?). I've been turned down by an introduction agency as too old (at 45), then found another which let me slip under the wire.

Finally, back on the singles scene again many years later, it was time to turn to the internet sites. Over the years, I've met and had relationships with men that have lasted for several years, for a few months, for a week or so, or not at all. I've gritted my teeth, brushed my hair, dusted off the decent shoes, and braved it out to meet a more or less total stranger for a drink, or a meal, or even a trip to the cinema. I've listened to their stories, laughed a bit, gone home to cry sometimes and got mad when I ran up a parking ticket on a date that went nowhere. More recently I met the new man in my life by going on holiday alone, feeling terribly depressed at being single, and allowing him to chat me up in a café in southern Italy. How bizarre and random is that? But when you read on, you'll come to my theories on random selection and how important it is that we make the pool in which this selection is to take place as large as possible.

You have to give fate a chance!

One of the problems when we discuss dating is that it covers a wide variety of hopes, expectations, desires and needs in different men and women. Some might be looking for flings, for a lot of sexual fun and excitement, no strings attached. Others are seriously looking for their mate in life, to get married and start a family. Others are secretly hoping to find a long-term partner, without the emphasis on a live-in 24/7 lifestyle.

This book concentrates on the more serious end of the spectrum, where women and men are looking for real relationships rather than sexual 'hook-ups'. And I'm proud that it's the *Ultimate Guide*, because I really want to help and make you appreciate that there is a lot of life out there for the living. Just read it through and you should emerge a lot wiser and more wised up. It should give you some hints and tips to turn what might have been a daunting prospect into something much more fun and easy to live with.

We'll look into personality typing and how to approach dating sensibly, looking for your 'compatible' match. We'll work on your nervousness, faults, fears and how to cope with all that. There's a lot of stories and advice on dealing with and how to get the best out of the various internet dating sites. Then we turn to look at the new methods of 'offline' dating that are springing up all the time. Moving on, you can read about how to get to go on that first date. And what to do afterwards if it was a success and you'd like to see more of him or her. Finally, just so you are streetwise and to show you know what you're talking about, there's a final chapter on the ins and outs of the business, so you don't have to listen to gossip or rumour any more. The back of the book is packed with useful resources, links to online dating sites galore and also to other forms of dating that have their own websites for promotion.

For now, happy reading and good luck with your dating adventures.

Chapter 1

What Sort of Dating Type are You?

Dating type – how can there be a dating type? Isn't that rather like asking what sort of lover or partner you would also make? Surely if we were all deeply rounded, and grounded, then we'd know much more about ourselves and wouldn't be in this pickle of trying to find a partner anyway.

First rule: don't beat yourself up over the fact you're out there in the dating and mating world. As I've already explained, so are millions of others. And those who aren't, well maybe they're the ones you should be feeling sorry for. In the adult western world, there are four basic groups if we are to consider the mating world as a whole (I've omitted those who are deliberately celibate on religious or philosophical grounds):

- The happily married or partnered who have no intention of looking for anyone else.
- The unhappily married or partnered, who are open to

themselves that they are into affairs, or sex on the side. They might move on, but most likely will stay with the status quo.

- The singles who would really like to meet someone special to be in their lives and who are actively dating.
- The singles who have basically given up on the whole scenario, can't stand any more of the pain and rejection, who figure a life of friends, work and companionship is fulfilling enough and that it's easier to forget about 'love, romance or sex'.

In this book, I am aiming my words at the third group, though no doubt some of the second will also sneak in under the wire.

Building your own mini-team

Dating is the first step in relationship-making. Relationships require two people who ultimately will form a mini-team, so that the two partners hopefully complement (not compliment, although that helps too!) each other's personality, character and attitudes.

One good way to approach the dating scene is to think of your dating life and adventures on a par with being a coach, or a manager, trying to put together the most effective team. You're looking for someone who will work well alongside you, bring out your creativity, whose faults or blemishes you can tolerate, or forgive, and who won't drive you mad after you've spent several days together. But, also, most importantly, someone who will set your heartstrings a-zinging.

Why should all this be so hard? In the world of business development and management training, many of us will already have come across 'personality profiling', such as the Myers-Briggs Type Indicator (MBTI™) or other variants. You might have previously worked on your own profile and deduced whether you could be described as, for example, an extrovert, introvert, leader, plodder, negotiator, pacifier, critic or wild child. I shall be talking more about the MBTI soon, as the theories have come to dominate a large part of the current dating scene. What holds for the management boardroom, it turns out also holds true in the dating arena.

Right now, I want to look at the obstacles that face any normal man or woman who is simply searching for that 'good fit' partner. Most people on the dating scene, unless they're no more than 14 years old, will have had some form of major disappointment already notched up. You may have been in love: it might have lasted a short time, or several years, but the final dissolution of that bond will have been just as devastating. Now you find yourself doubting your ability to choose a 'suitable' person to be in your life. You may have had many girl or boyfriends but so far love has eluded you. You might even wonder what people mean by falling in love – why don't you hear the bells ringing and the birds singing? Why does finding someone special seem so difficult? Anyone you even mildly fancy seems to turn away as though you were a speck of dust on the carpet.

So what gets in the way of rational choice?

Here are a few pointers that I've put together from my own experience. Maybe you can add more?

- We want to meet a special person and, even more, to be bowled over by falling in love. But it's impossible to guess ahead of meeting that 'him' or 'her' what type of person we might fall for. For most, it could be that a type of hair colouring, body build, height, weight, look, smile, character, ability to laugh, ability to cite Shakespeare, or a certain look in the eyes, is what most turns us on. Yet that will never hold true in a global way. Where one person with that kind of appearance can set the heart racing, a similar body build or colouring, or knowing the dictionary backwards match will leave us cold.
- Chemistry is the hidden ingredient, and there is no real way of assessing from a written description, or photo, or high recommendation from family or friends, whether the person will create the necessary spark. I've often thought there should be a global DNA bank whereby we can run our own genetic material through a million tests with zillions of others to find the 'perfect match'. Or maybe it should be a pheromone bank. Very often, when we talk of chemistry, we mean that the smell, taste, or even the sweat of another person is the ingredient that creates that amazingly powerful attraction, makes the palms sweat and the knees tremble.

- For some, the potential for attraction may be grounded in more rational, or commercial/commodity-like expectations. Perhaps for you, chemistry is less important than the size of a man's bank balance, the amplitude of a woman's breasts, or the stunning movie-star-like appearance of a much younger woman or man.
- Yet the bedrock of all problems, beneath any of the surface reasons, is that old spoiler: your self-esteem, level of self-confidence, anxiety about your appearance, fear of rejection and abandonment, and an inability to know what type of person you really are looking for. These are the out-of-control emotions that make dating such a challenge for many of us.

I'll move on to discuss more on those tricky topics in Chapter 2, 'Prepare Yourself for Dating'.

••••••••••

'Just looking at a photo or even staring at women across a crowded room doesn't begin to say anything about what she might be like or whether she'd find me attractive.'

Chris is a really nice, interesting man in his late-40s, who has been on his own since his marriage of over 20 years broke down, about five or six years ago. When he was married, and a captain of industry, he never had a problem with women. They'd find him attractive and vice versa. But now, after several years of singlehood and dating in all its guises, he feels like a misfit in today's world. He spends a lot of time and thought analysing the situation.

> *I've tried giving myself a test looking at women in groups together when I'm out socially, or at their photos on different online sites, to see if I have a 'type' that I find attractive. The truth is that it doesn't work. Just looking at a photo or even staring at women across a crowded room doesn't begin to say anything about what she might be like or whether she'd find me attractive. That's why I find it so hard and the longer it goes on, it's easier to withdraw and retreat back into the solitary life at home. Except then I get fed up going out on my own and I'm back out there, hope and expectations ready again for battle!*

• • • • • • • • • • •

Why do sparks fly with one person and not another?

Falling in love is not just about sexual attraction or even finding someone you're sexually compatible with. It's about finding someone who lightens up your life, who excites you at the same time as making you want to care for them. The chemistry of 'love' is often written about – mainly because no one has yet managed to bottle the secret elixir or tell us how to go out and find that certain someone. I'm sure that for most of us, if we were to go to a relationship counsellor, an introduction agency, or find ourselves writing a profile for one of the many online dating sites, it wouldn't take long before we were saying, 'I know more or less the type of person I'm looking for, but even if he/she checks the normal social and mutual interest boxes, there still has to be that spark for me to take it further …' As we all know, just liking someone is not a strong enough driver to bring out the rapture of romantic love.

How does the yearning to fall in love fit in the 'dating game'? The truth is that unless you are a very practical person, and just want to find a 'decent enough mate', this yearning will dominate your search.

It might mean that you expect to be immediately bowled over by him or her; want to be able to walk into a crowded room, lock eyes, and just know that this person is for you. Or, slightly more sensibly, you might feel that if he/she makes you laugh, has a twinkle in the eye, and at least checks some of the boxes, then that's good enough for now. If you get along well on the first and second date, you won't let yourself go until you've had that first kiss. If that works, then the likelihood is everything else will. But if the kiss is dead, or lifeless, or you don't like the taste or smell of him/her, then there's not much point in taking it further.

Even more strongly, you might say that even if the kiss is great, you would make sure you went to bed together quite early on. If the electricity doesn't zing when you have sex, then that's it.

Ouch! Dating and mating can be painful. But the prize at the end of the search is so enticing, most people continue to pick themselves up, dust themselves off, and start all over again.

Most in the psychological profession believe we fall in love with someone who fits an inner set of traits that we are seeking in a partner, but these traits are known only at a subconscious level. We are programmed to mate, to have sex, so that the race multiplies and some of us become mothers and fathers. Romantic love is the beginning of that drive, and is very different from the basic sex drive (that's the drive for the fun and satisfaction from sex totally unrelated to being in love).

Romantic love is what makes us want to stay with a partner either for life, or at least for enough years to see the offspring raised and ready to leave the nest on their own two feet. We similarly tend to feel 'romantic love' for our children when they are born, which gives us sufficient energy and commitment to struggle through the sleepless nights and impoverished days of early childcare. The intense, almost overwhelming love we feel for a newborn is not dissimilar to the overpowering force of amazement when we fall in love with another adult. You might see this new love's face, or a baby's, in your mind's eye as a towering force, which is a very graphic manifestation of the power of love. It's maybe also why the most often used term of endearment for the person we love is 'baby'. We're not saying we want them to be baby-like (or not all of us!), but we want to love them as much as we might our newborn infant.

There is no escape from the fact that falling in love, or being in love – the rapture, the excitement of knowing another person, the most significant person in our small world – is one of the great 'highs' of life. It's better than drink or drugs or winning the lottery. Some people, of course, find themselves addicted to this high, which comes from a release of the opiate-like brain chemicals, dopamine and serotonin. That addiction in itself can lead to yet more millions joining the dating game, as love in a previous marriage or relationship begins to wither on the vine after several years and the urge to fall in love again takes hold, leading to another round of divorces. There wouldn't be many novels of great passion and love if man or woman was never challenged by meeting a new love and having to pursue the course of togetherness against all the odds.

Here's my own list of some of the hidden traits we might be looking for in another person, which lie deep beneath the obvious. So, where you might be stating that the person you are looking for must have dark/fair hair; GSOH; work in similar profession or industry – the check boxes and lists we tend to make for ourselves in hunting for a mate – the real driving force might be whether:

- We are drawn to another because we share some deep-hidden flaw. If you felt rejected by your mother or father as a child, for example, then you are quite likely to fall for a partner who has undergone similar negative experiences.
- You have a fear of intimacy or are a commitment-phobe and find yourself continually attracted to men or women who back away, thereby turning you into the one who chases or appears needy. In fact their behaviour is a mirror image of your own.

- You are attracted by similarity, either of social background or at least of 'values'. This is especially true for men and women who have an overriding interest in one particular area of the world outside – politics, art, music and sport being among the obvious.
- You might be attracted by someone different, along the lines of the old adage 'opposites attract'. If mystery or exoticism is what turns you on, then there is not much point in trying to date the 'boy/girl next door type'.

Whoever we meet and fall in love with (unless we live by the principles of an arranged marriage) will be the result of 'random selection'. You might disagree, saying, 'That can't be so, as I fell in love with the boy next door.' But even that meeting or bringing together of two people was down to circumstance: your parents moved into the same street as the parents of your boyfriend. Either set of parents might have chosen to live in a different town – would you then have met each other?

The randomness of falling in love

Fate and destiny play a large part in the mating game and, as we know, most new lovers tend to marvel at the strange circumstances that have brought them together. Whether you met on board an ocean liner; bumped into each other on the London Tube; gazed at each other over the computers in your office; eyed each other up in a bar when one group of friends introduced you to another group; were formally introduced through an agency; or met through an online dating site, destiny played a card to make sure you were both there, at the same time, and were able to meet.

Whether you were attracted to someone very similar to you – in terms of social background, views, beliefs, love of sport or dancing – or felt the excitement coming from someone who is very different from you in most things, the driving cause of the attraction will have come from two sets of very individual inner motivators.

Meeting someone through what biologists would call 'random selection' means you have to find large groups from which you can choose. This is the main reason why 'internet dating' has taken off and become so widely popular. The 'dating' itself has nothing to do with the internet. Speed dating works from the same concept, but as the meeting involves face-to-face sessions, the potential numbers available are understandably lower.

The internet has provided the opportunity to meet or be introduced to a much wider circle of people than you would naturally ever meet. It ups the ante on random selection and, just maybe, shortens the odds that destiny will play you a winning card. If the chance of randomly meeting someone with whom you might fall in love can be as remote as 1 in 40,000, then enabling your access to hundreds or even thousands of other human beings should be helping destiny along its way.

Here are a few happy examples of how this 'randomness' can work.

●●●●●●●●●●●

'I was the first and only person he met through the site!'

Linda and Barry are the sort of couple who seem to have found love very easily, when they both decided in their separate ways to sign up to an online site. Five years ago, when they were in their early-30s, they both started looking for someone at the same time. They worked not far from each other in London. But there is no way they could ever have met. They signed up individually to www.wheresmydate.com, at a time when internet dating was seen as far more risqué than it is now. Where Linda is talkative and outgoing, Barry, an economist who works for a think tank, is quiet, shy and tends to the introspective. They share very strong views about the world and their interests.

Linda: *I felt like I was taking control of my life, rather than waiting to see if something would happen. Barry was only the second person I met. For him, I was the first and only person he met through the site! I was working for a disability charity and my co-workers logged me on. To us, it was a bit of a laugh. I'm quite a happy-go-lucky type and very sociable, so it was no problem to me. But Barry is shy and reserved. We hit it off straightaway. We're both educated, political and serious-minded. We'd written about our politics in the profiles, being pretty left wing, and about our love of music and film. I think the way you see the world is very important. We're both people who try to live our lives by certain values.*

After nine months of going out, we were starting to talk of living together. We seemed to have realised at the same time that this was 'it' for us. On holiday in Ireland, we came to a decision to get married. Now we still can't believe it, because we're so happy together. We might have remained stuck in our rooms, alone and single, if either of us had not made the move to meet someone new!

• • • • • • • • • • •

'As we got to know more about each other, it began to feel like destiny.'

Kathy and Mark are another couple who seem to have known what they were looking for, and found each other almost effortlessly. Kathy married young at 25, having met her first husband just after graduating. She was married for five years, but that broke up very suddenly two years ago. Mark works in IT for a major bank. He'd been with one woman for many years, and when that relationship ended, he tried living on his own for a time, but turning 40, made a New Year's resolution to do something about his situation. He was almost resigned to living on his own, and had begun to give up on ever finding a permanent girlfriend.

Kathy: *I hadn't dated anyone properly since I was a teenager and the thought of starting out from scratch filled me with dread. Most of my friends were in long-term relationships or married. I'm quite shy and just hated the thought of it all. I couldn't imagine having to talk to strangers in a bar. Besides that I was living in Paris at the time. Being in Paris made things even more difficult, because despite the image of that city, socially it's very different from London (or New York). You don't tend to make close friends of your colleagues. They're very family-oriented and go home in the evenings. One weekend, I was with a gay friend who told me about an amazing gay online dating site, and he encouraged me to go online.*

That evening on Eurostar, I drafted out my profile for a site, calling myself 'eurostar'. I took a quick photo of myself in the flat and uploaded it. Can you believe that the next day Mark contacted me? He'd seen my profile and wanted to get in touch straightaway. He works in London and I was back in Paris, so we emailed a lot from March to April. Whenever I was back in London we'd meet. But towards the end of May we got together as a couple. It was a real whirlwind romance and we moved in together in November.

I couldn't believe at first that he'd chosen me! He's nice-looking, in a high-powered City career, earns a good salary, is nine years older than me and never married. He's also a linguist, fluent in French and German, speaks Japanese, which I've always wanted to learn. We were both looking for someone to marry and start a family. At first it all seemed too good to be true. I couldn't quite believe it. But as we got to know more about each other, it also began to feel like destiny. Our lives had crossed many times. He was at university in the city I lived in when I was taking my A levels. We could have been on the same street and met all those years ago!

●●●●●●●●●●

How to find out your personality profile

Did you notice in those profiles that the word 'shy' cropped up in both? And the partners they have fallen in love with are not so shy? Inevitably the shy, or those naturally more introspective, might find the process of going out, proactively hunting for a potential mate or dating partner, to be an excruciating prospect. Whereas a more extroverted, outgoing, happy-go-lucky type might be much more at ease in the general social scene, not too concerned about the chat-up potential of being in bars, going to clubs or parties. But shy or introspective people do not necessarily want to meet only those with the same tendencies, just as not all extroverts want to date equally loquacious or outward-going partners.

There are other ways of trying to narrow down the field, so that you get to meet or date potentially suitable men or women, who might just become that special someone. One of the first questions to find out about yourself is what sort of 'dating type' you most closely match, so that you can try to meet similar types. So now let's look at the move that personality type testing has recently made, from the business world to the dating arena.

If you have come across the Myers-Briggs Type Indicator (MBTI™) questionnaire in the workplace for team building, maybe you won't be surprised that they are now being used extensively for dating. Many men and women already know their type, either from having run the test in the office, or by taking a related quiz in a self-help book, or on an online dating site, and they have started to use the acronyms when seeking a dating partner. For example, 'thoughtful ISTJ seeks similar'. Because rather than just focus on the fact you are either shy or outward-going, the MBTI will give you a much more rounded view of your total personality profile. And this just might be the clue to finding a compatible partner.

I'm not going to spend hours here going into the detail of a Myers-Briggs assessment, as readers can research it more fully in their own time, for example by looking into sites such as these: www.teamtechnology.co.uk and www.win.net/insights/personality_frames.htm.

But if you glance over the 16 different types, you might immediately come away with a sense of who you are, or where you fit in the personality spectrum. Do make sure to read the notes that explain how in Myers-Briggs the terms are not to be interpreted as we might normally use them. They are shorthand for describing a quite complex analysis of personality and attitudes. If you want to pursue the use of personality testing further, there are a couple of US-based internet sites – www.TypeTango.com and www.JungDate.com – that set up matches according to the Myers-Briggs assessment. There are UK and European sites that have devised their own personality profiling, which you might also find fun to explore. More on them soon.

• • • • • • • • • • •

'He wanted women to see him at his worst!'

So, you're out to look for compatibility not sameness. This story of Jenni and Tom, very romantic and inspiring as it is, really tells the tale about how we might not know what we are looking for. Yet when it turns up on the doorstep, even if you're not bowled over instantly, at a certain point you realise this is the right person for you. And, more importantly, why – because you complement each other.

Jenni is nearly 40, living in London, and holds down a high-powered (well, at least very time-consuming) job in marketing. Having met and enjoyed talking to her one evening, I can also say she's stunningly good-looking and you'd never put her age at anywhere near the big four-0. Outgoing, friendly, warm, I assumed, 'Surely she has tons of boyfriends, why would she need to go online?' Jenni explains:

> *I went on to the* Guardian's *Soulmates site (www.guardiansoulmates.com) as I am an avid reader and I'd heard they have a lot of really interesting people on the site, who politically would probably be on the same wavelength as me.*

One of the first people to respond to my profile was Tom. I remember he wrote saying he should get in quick before I was inundated. I did get a large immediate response, about 48 emails.

I tried to be honest in my profile and said that 'I prefer still waters that run deep.' About a prospective man, that I wanted to meet someone who is into food, music, adventures and other cultures. I was also brave, adding I'd like him to be sexually experienced.

Tom's username was 'Ozbound', as he was (and is) planning to emigrate to Australia. He wrote that although he'd be leaving the country in a year or so's time, he'd like to meet some quality women for company. When I met Jenni, they were applying for a partner visa so she will accompany him.

Because he was going away, some of the pressure seemed to have been removed. I didn't really have to take him seriously. He'd put an awful photo of himself on the site, squinting into the sun. He says that he wanted women to see him at his worst! He was never what I would have described as my type, being slender, blond, just a bit taller than me (and 18 months younger). He's from the Midlands and works in the techie world. But he does love food and cooking. I went to Cambridge University, have a Masters degree, and speak several languages. On paper, I'm super-duper. But in reality I'm just Me. He is equally bright, just not so formally educated.

Tom really is my perfect match in temperament. He's calm, steady and supportive, yet he can be the party animal too. We had six months to get to know each other slowly, until he was meant to leave. Looking back, fortunately the paperwork was delayed. Until this past May, I was totally undecided about him. Then we went to Morocco on holiday. It was fun until I got very sick on my final day and all through the night. It was food poisoning and it felt like I was about to die. Our flight was in the morning and I just knew there was no hanging about, I wanted to get home. He carried the heavy bags, stayed calm throughout, got me home and made sure I was OK. He didn't over-egg the situation or worry too much. I liked that.

A week later, suddenly I realised I'd fallen in love with him. It became obvious we wanted to continue being together. That's when the possibility of my emigrating to Australia with him came up, and we agreed to live together. He moved from Hackney into my Kensington flat.

Now we're living together and it turns out we're so well suited. Before him I'd been looking for someone like me, rather literary and postgrad-educated. I've never felt so relaxed. We support and complement each other. He makes me feel truly loved. And he seems much happier than he used to be.

Why did he choose me? Tom says that when he saw my profile as it first went up he had to email me straightaway. 'You seemed sussed. You had a beautiful photo and I liked what you'd written, especially the line "I love life, even though it does sometimes do my head in." You seemed incredible, a bit out of my league but I thought I'd give it a try anyway.'

• • • • • • • • • •

What's your type?

The types identified by Myers-Briggs are:

ENFJ – Extroverted iNtuitive Feeling Judger

ENFP – Extroverted iNtuitive Feeling Perceiver

ENTJ – Extroverted iNtuitive Thinking Judger

ENTP – Extroverted iNtuitive Thinking Perceiver

ESFJ – Extroverted Sensing Feeling Judger

ESFP – Extroverted Sensing Feeling Perceiver

ESTJ – Extroverted Sensing Thinking Judger

ESTP – Extroverted Sensing Thinking Perceiver

INFJ – Introverted iNtuitive Feeling Judger

INFP – Introverted iNtuitive Feeling Perceiver

INTJ – Introverted iNtuitive Thinking Judger

INTP – Introverted iNtuitive Thinking Perceiver

ISFJ – Introverted Sensing Feeling Judger

ISFP – Introverted Sensing Feeling Perceiver

ISTJ – Introverted Sensing Thinking Judger

ISTP – Introverted Sensing Thinking Perceiver

Extroverted/Introverted – means where we most focus our energy. Extroverts are usually stimulated by being with people. Introverts are inspired by quiet reflection and prefer to recharge alone.

Sensing/Intuitive – refers to how we take in information. The sensors among us may prefer tangible data and rely on their five senses. Intuitives are attracted by concepts or abstract ideas and trust their sixth sense.

Thinking/Feeling – looks at how we make decisions. Thinkers are drawn towards things logical and analytical. They see things in terms of principles. Feelers are more visceral, emotional and see things in terms of personal values.

Judging/Perceiving – this looks at how we approach life. Judgers may prefer structure, defined goals and decisions. Perceivers like to keep their options open and explore possibilities.

The Myers-Briggs Type Indicator (MBTI™) was devised by Isabel Briggs Myers and her mother Katharine Cook Briggs in the mid-1950s, based on some of the writings of Carl Jung. It is still going strong and some 2 million people fill out the questionnaires on an annual basis. The important point about its applicability to dating is that there are no right or wrong answers. *We are all very different human beings and no one type is better or worse than another.*

Other agencies, online or offline, may use slightly different terminology. For example, another version (on www.chemistry.com) offers four main personality types, described as the Explorer, the Builder, the Negotiator and the Director, again mixing our profile in the workplace with that in the dating arena.

The Builder is someone who is calm, dependable and thorough, who shines at executive and managerial skills, either at work or in the home. The type of person might be happiest dating someone who is impulsive and a risk-taker.

The Explorer is someone who loves to discover new things, new ideas, travel, etc. They might be very spontaneous and do things on the spur of the moment, also having a strong sense of adventure. In dating, they would likely be most attracted to a similar like-minded personality.

The Negotiator is intuitive and understanding, very much a people-person, who is tuned in to how others think and feel. Often charming and tactful, they could be attracted to a variety of personality types.

The Director might be highly inventive, very determined and competitive; a decision-maker and often a dynamic leader at work. However, that competitive spirit might be difficult for a romantic partner.

Personality profiling can make match-makers of us all

Introduction agency counsellors involved in interviewing men and women clients on a one-to-one basis use 'match-making' skills, most likely derived from their own intuitive understanding of who would get along well with Mr X and who would find Ms Y really stimulating company. An agency would be unlikely to put two bold extrovert personalities together, for fear they would not get a word in edgeways with each other. Similarly, personality-profiling questionnaires that appear with some frequency on online dating sites are trying to mimic those intuitive skills that came naturally to dear old grandmothers in the village hall when the local dance was taking place.

What I really want to make clear is that these categorisations share pretty much the same basic information. Each of us will have a few basic personality and attitude traits. So, rather than looking to find someone who is exactly the same, what we should be focusing on is searching for a compatible partner, who will best complement our strengths and weaknesses. Less fighting, more understanding and forgiveness.

In Europe, personality matching and testing as a way of encouraging daters to focus on real-live possibilities is increasing, at least at the top end of the market. Face-to-face introduction agencies, and internet dating sites that ask you to fill out 80-plus questions, then pay for the report afterwards, are obviously going to appeal more to the man or woman who: a) can afford the cost and the time involved; and b) is much more serious about wanting to find a true mate, rather than a quick fling. It's a rather sweet return to old-fashioned values, in the love and mating arena, whereby we are allowing some of the old match-making skills to return and help shift the presence of destiny in our lives.

Inevitably, the online dating sites are producing the majority of the personality profiling, as the questionnaire lends itself to computer interactivity and the user has more time and space to enter into this world of cross-matching than would be possible in the 'offline' dating arena. Speed dating agencies do try and group men and women in age group, location and possible like-minded areas such as professional background. But, after that, you are on your own to guess at someone else's personality type.

How to find that truly compatible partner

For now we have to ask forgiveness from the other forms of dating provider and take another peek into the personality profiling, more European-style, as offered by online dating agencies in the United Kingdom and Europe: sites such as www.loveandfriends.co.uk or the even more intensive www.parship.co.uk. The latter claims to have 2 million members across Europe, though the UK figure is somewhat lower at 400,000. The 83-item Parship questionnaire is offered free, but to access the equally long report you need to sign up and pay for membership. The questionnaire is a hybrid mix of the theories of Jung, Freud and some Myers-Briggs. The questions, based on 30 basic readings of our possible personalities, have been tested on a broad selection of people and, as one who has taken the test and read the report with fascination, I rather liked its no-nonsense approach.

The process of selecting a partner is a highly complicated interaction of senses, first impressions, patterns of conversation and basic character traits. It is not something that can be summarised in a few bare facts or statistics. In order to find a partner who is a good match for you, you first need a clear picture of your own strengths and weaknesses. Only those who know themselves thoroughly and objectively will be able to recognise a complementary partner when they meet him or her. But of course realistic self-evaluation is an elusive commodity – it is hard to achieve on our own.

In the long run, if we sit down and really think these things through, a relationship between two people is more likely to succeed if there is a balance between the head, heart and instinct, features that have been identified as basic patterns of behaviour common to all of us: the battle between being driven by reason, feeling or instinct. For example, if one partner demonstrates a tendency towards rational decision making, that person would be best matched with a partner who knows how to use his or her instinct as a counterbalance.

Reading the report on the results of my questionnaire helped me get to know myself a bit better. Parship defines goals in slightly different terms from classic MBTI. It tests on introversion, extroversion, social adaptability, and inhibition towards social interaction. I learnt that a norm is taken from all Parship interviews, which have been run with a variety of people, and personality traits and attitudes are scored against this norm. The easiest people to match are the ones who make up the average point: down the middle, Mr and Ms Average. Those with more strongly held views, passions or obsessions are harder to match. And guess what? I came out on the 'strongly held views' side. What a surprise! If you're a writer, it's pretty hard not to have strong views, or what would you have to write about?

Putting myself down at first for these rather Attila-like tendencies, I was intrigued by the following comment. I may not quite match the high-earning category, but yes, I can see the point about the rest of the description:

> *If you're a woman, in a high-earning career, with a strong personality, we wouldn't match you to an alpha male, but maybe to someone who is more in touch with his feminine side. It doesn't mean there is anything intrinsically wrong with you, but being outside of the average band might reduce the number of potential matches.*

So here is some of what I recently learnt about myself. I have a very strong 'animus', which means I score too low in the 'typically feminine' areas. That's OK: as someone who grew up during the feminist period, I'm quite comfortable with such an assessment. It is not only women who possess the so-called 'feminine' qualities, and the so-called 'masculine' qualities are not only found in men. There are 'masculine' traits hidden in every woman, and vice versa. Research by the Swiss psychologist C G Jung (1875–1961) has shown that successful relationships are characterised by balanced proportions of these qualities in equal measure.

Clichés abound when it comes to describing masculine or feminine characteristics. Warmth, sensitivity, gentleness, weakness, sentimentalism, reason, strength, objectivity, obstinacy, rudeness or the desire for power – all of these have been described at one time or another as 'typically masculine' or 'typically feminine' characteristics. But when it comes to psychological significance, the reality is more complicated.

In short, the 'feminine' psychological category refers to attributes like outward expression of feeling, a dependence on mood and intuition and a sensitivity to events which impact on the inner lives of friends and acquaintances. The 'masculine' category is associated with initiative, courage and rational deduction.

As I have said earlier, a site that uses such a complex questionnaire, and expects quite a lot of thought and effort in putting together your personal profile or description of yourself, and of the type of person you are looking for, is very much a relationship-oriented agency. This kind of online dating site, along with more traditional introduction agencies, is asking you to put your money where your mouth is.

You will not be exposed to thousands of photos of would-be daters, but are sent at first the top ten matches, those to whom you are most psychometrically suited (according to the computer). Your top three might score a match base as high as 85 per cent, but anything over 65 per cent is seen as strong potential. Because there are no photos involved at first, you the client have to work harder, take time to read the profiles, and the personality and compatibility reports. It's not like being chatted up in a bar!

Where to go from here

So you are beginning to understand yourself a little better. You've built up at least a small grasp of your overall personality type and the complementary personality you might be looking for in a partner. If you're a natural-born extrovert, you may not have too many problems with the dating game, whereas if you are shy and introverted, it can prove more challenging. Even Kathy, whose story we read earlier, now happily with Mark, expecting their first child and soon to be married, confessed that her natural-born shyness and horror at the prospect of going back on the dating scene, which she had not done since her teenage years, meant that when she was introduced to the internet dating phenomenon suddenly her shyness was not such a problem:

> *I'm quite happy writing, rather than talking, so the prospect of writing about myself for the internet was appealing. I didn't find that in any way so embarrassing as having to meet people in bars. It also means you can screen people and decide who or not you might meet.*

What next? Now it's time to see whether you are ready to hit the dating scene, along with all those millions of other eager hopefuls. But first take this quiz, which is an easy way to sum up quite a lot of what we have been talking about. Are you brave and enterprising, keen to get out there on the hunt? Or shy and retiring, preferring a nice cup of tea and your favourite TV programme? Neither style is right or wrong. They just point up the differences. Good luck!

Quiz

How far would you go to get a date?

1. *Imagine a single friend of yours suggests you both try speed dating. Would you be up for it?*
   a) Definitely. In fact I'd be the one suggesting it in the first place.
   b) Yes I think so. It wouldn't do any harm and it would probably be a laugh.
   c) Probably. I think I would give it a go if he or she arranged it all.
   d) Probably not. I'd have to be really desperate.
   e) Definitely not. It's not my sort of thing and quite frankly, I couldn't think of anything worse.

2. *You travel to work on the Tube. Most days for the last two weeks, a good-looking guy/girl has been at your station and you've exchanged glances. It's got to the point where you've smiled at each other and looked away. He/she looks like the sort of person you'd like to go on a date with. What would you do?*
   a) I think I'd be too shy to do anything.
   b) Two weeks? You must be joking – I'd have gone up and talked to him/her the second time we bumped into each other.
   c) I'd try looking and smiling a bit more the next time we saw each other and see what sort of response I got.
   d) If I fancied him/her, I'd go and strike up a conversation – nothing ventured, nothing gained.

e) I'd ask him/her out for a coffee or drink after work.

3. *There's someone at work that you've fancied for a while. You like the way he/she looks, dresses and seems really confident and funny when he/she has to give a presentation. You know he/she's single but the trouble is that you've never had the chance to get to know each other, except just to say hello. Could you pursue things?*
a) I'd just put it to the back of my mind. It's no good to get distracted by things like that at work.
b) I'd think about it, but unless we worked with each other directly, I don't think I could do anything about it.
c) I'd tell a trusted colleague who knew him/her and hope that the word got back.
d) I'd make an effort with my appearance if I thought we'd bump into each other that day and then make a couple of glances in his/her direction, hoping I might catch his/her eye.
e) I'd catch him/her at a quiet moment and suggest we go out for a drink some time.
f) I'd make a good effort to chat and flirt if I could and see how it went.

4. *You're in a trendy bar with a few friends one Friday night. You've seen someone there who's caught your eye and really stands out for you. He/she looks just your type. What would you do?*
a) Get one of my friends to go over to say I fancy him/her.

b) Do nothing.

c) Confidently sit back and let him/her come to me.

d) Try and make eye contact to see if I can get his/her attention.

e) Get my friends to stand right near him/her so that it's easier for a conversation to get started.

f) Go up and ask if I can buy him/her a drink or some other excuse to directly chat him/her up.

5. *You've got to know an ex-colleague of yours quite well, say for at least six months. You've become good friends and you often text each other or meet up for a coffee or for lunch. So far it's just been completely platonic as he/she was seeing someone else for the first two months. You've fancied him/her since you first met and the connection has grown since then, but there's no obvious flirtation. How would you handle this situation?*

a) I think if there's a true friendship, I wouldn't want to ruin things so I'd just keep things as they were.

b) I'd just tell him/her how I felt and take it from there.

c) I'd tell him/her that I'd been in love since we first met.

d) I'd arrange to go out in the evening instead, get us both drunk and jump on him/her.

e) I'd love to be able to progress things but I'd be too shy, so I'd just keep hoping that he/she would do something about it.

f) I'd make a subtle suggestion like 'Do you know, I've always though you'd make someone a great boyfriend/girlfriend' and see what sort of response I got.

6. *If you became newly single or recently decided that you'd like to meet someone, would you put the word out to everyone you knew?*

   a) I don't think I'd go round telling people that I'd like to meet someone, even good friends, as I wouldn't want to appear desperate.

   b) I'd tell a few good friends so that we could go for a few nights out together.

   c) I'd send emails to my friends, family and non-work contacts asking for them to suggest potential dates for me.

   d) I'd mention it to a few friends to see if they knew anyone they could set me up with, perhaps for a blind date.

7. *Would you try internet dating?*

   a) Yes, I have done and I have gone on dates with people I've met on the internet.

   b) I've signed up to internet dating services but not gone on any dates.

   c) I'd think about it, but only if I'd been single for quite a while and hadn't met anyone through the traditional routes.

   d) Possible but unlikely.

   e) Definitely not.

   f) I'd definitely give it a try if I'd been single for a while.

8. *Would you chat to a stranger in the supermarket?*
   a) Definitely. I've found it pays to speak to as many people as you can, whether they're a potential date or not.
   b) Yes. It's worked for me. I've been on at least one date with someone I've met in the supermarket.
   c) I would chat to people briefly, but only if they started the conversation first.
   d) I'd chat briefly or make the odd comment, but I'd be too intimidated to do the same with someone I found attractive who could be suitable date material.
   e) No. I tend to just get on with my shopping and go.

9. *How many first dates have you been on in the last 12 months?*
   a) None
   b) 1
   c) 2 or 3
   d) 4 or 5
   e) 6 to 10
   f) More than 10

Your answers

1. a) 4 b) 3 c) 2 d) 1 e) 0
2. a) 0 b) 4 c) 2 d) 3 e) 4
3. a) 0 b) 1 c) 3 d) 2 e) 4 f) 3
4. a) 3 b) 0 c) 1 d) 2 e) 3 f) 4
5. a) 0 b) 4 c) 5 d) 3 e) 0 f) 2
6. a) 0 b) 2 c) 4 d) 3
7. a) 4 b) 3 c) 2 d) 1 e) 0 f) 3

8. a) 3 b) 4 c) 2 d) 1 e) 0
9. a) 0 b) 0 c) 1 d) 2 e) 3 f) 4

Scoring

You can't help acting on impulse (31–37)

You've got a lot of bottle. The thought of chatting up a stranger, or anyone for that matter, doesn't seem to bother you much. You might not get a 100 per cent hit rate, but the thought of rejection bothers you much less than the prospect of not trying in the first place. You probably have the confidence to carry it off most of the time, which can be an attractive quality, but be sure that you don't comes across as too arrogant if you don't want to put off those who might be more sensitive than you. After all, it's flattering that someone finds you so attractive that they'd chat you up, even in a supermarket, but no one wants to feel that you do this sort of thing all the time.

Brave but not brash (24–30)

You're confident enough to go for it in most circumstances, but there are certain lines you wouldn't cross. You wouldn't want to make a complete fool of yourself, but you're willing to take a risk when it comes to getting a date. This attitude is likely to pay off eventually and it's likely it has done in the past many times already. Keep up the good work, but don't be too pushy with it.

Could do better (10–23)

You'd be willing to go out of your way a little bit to get a date, but not too much. You prefer to work along subtle lines of approach. Perhaps you're just too shy, perhaps you just hate the thought of rejection or maybe you've just accepted a single way of life. Perhaps chatting up a stranger in the supermarket might be going a bit far for you, but why not try chatting to people more every day – on your daily commute, in the shops or when you're at work? It doesn't have to be someone you'd like to ask out on a date, but it builds your confidence and might brighten your day. Also you could give internet dating a try. It's grown hugely in popularity in the last couple of years and there's the added advantage of knowing you're likely to email someone who's also looking to meet someone.

Too shy for your own good (0–9)

Your shyness is definitely getting the better of you. If you've been single for a while, you should definitely think about broadening your horizons and just taking a tiny risk now and then. Make small talk with your colleagues more, even people you don't need to speak to every day about work, go speed dating with a friend and just treat it as an experience or, if you're really serious about meeting someone, give internet dating a try, but be proactive in the process and make the first move. What have you got to lose?

Chapter 2

Prepare Yourself for Dating

So what's the big deal then? You've given some thought to your personality type and what sort of personality might offer you a compatible partner. There are literally millions of single people worldwide; hundreds if not thousands of eager entrepreneurs in the background, creating ways for everyone to meet up, from online dating sites, to personal introduction agencies, to social networking operations that promote their events online – speed dating, dance dating, golf parties, bridge evenings and singles themed holidays. Surely you're not still finding this situation difficult? I bet you are! I know that in my own life, I have always found the actual dating at times cringe-makingly embarrassing.

The problem for most of us is one of sheer terror or confusion. How to launch yourself into that big scary world out there? How to calm your nerves, boost the flagging self-esteem and meet 'the love of your life' or a 'soul mate'? A lot of what has been written on this topic is fine in theory, but trying it out in practice can be a very different matter.

• • • • • • • • • • •

'I just didn't know how to meet someone new.'

Pauline, who is now in her late-30s, lively, bubbly and fortunately settled again with a boyfriend, looks back to the time when she was 33, working in London and newly single after a very long relationship had broken down.

> *All my friends bar two were married or in relationships. They're not the best girlfriends to go out with, as they have their commitments. I'd been with this one guy for 11 years and he suddenly left me. The first six months I was single, I was so happy! Then I became miserable because I just didn't know how to meet someone new. You'd meet a guy while you were out and go on a date, then discover he'd lied to you about not being married. It was awful. Another problem you find when you're in your 30s and early-40s is that compared to dating in your 20s, everyone now has baggage. Men and women have issues and that makes them different and not so appealing. The pool has also become smaller and you've got more fussy!*

• • • • • • • • • • •

Why we have to date

Pauline sums up a lot of the problems that most of us face as we embark on the business of 'dating'. Let's have a look at why we even have to date. Whatever happened to finding love, romance, or even friendship with a member of the opposite sex (or same sex if that is preferred) in what we still tend to feel is the 'natural' way? There is nothing to say that such an organic method won't or doesn't happen. It's just that it might take an awfully long time. Not many of us feel we want, or have the time, to wait that long.

We first start to fancy and maybe go out with people in our school days. This obviously increases dramatically as we reach our late teens and, for many, university or college is the heyday of romance, partnering, maybe trying out living together, or living in groups. For some, first marriages take place in our early 20s. The shock can come though when university or college days are over. First jobs, often in the rat race of building up a career, might lead to friendships with potential lovers, but now commerce, competition and sense have overtaken youthful hedonism. We're not so quick to settle with someone, after several years of experience. As Pauline says, we have all become fussier. Even worse, if an early marriage or living together arrangement then backfires, you find yourself out there on your own again. Maybe you have children. Even without children, you will have built up a level of baggage and some scars. You probably no longer feel like chatting up, or being the target of chat-up, in bars and clubs and have outgrown the supposed fun of going back home with a stranger, having sex, and wondering why you did that. So what else can you do if you find yourself single again?

In the west, we do not have arranged marriages. Your parents no doubt long ago gave up on trying to match you with the son or daughter of their dear (but to you very boring) friends. Churches don't hold the sway they used to. We don't live in small tight communities, wherein the local dance in the village hall was the match-making centre of that small universe. The workplace has become almost out of bounds as a place to form relationships. You might go to the gym once or twice a week, but can you imagine even talking to anyone there, other than to argue that you were next in line to be on the cross-trainer? Returning to my theme of random selection in Chapter 1, dating is vital to our post-20th-century lifestyles as a way of bringing people together and allowing the roulette wheel to turn (or dice to fall, if you prefer).

Yet still the concept of actively 'dating', proactively seeking out potential partners, by meeting them for a quick drink, for a movie, dinner in a restaurant, or in any other likely format, can seem cold, calculating and very stress-inducing. When we were younger, we might have talked about 'going out', or 'going steady' with someone. There just wasn't the concept that we got to market test the next available sample, on a ten-day free trial or return basis.

This is the basis of the world we live in now, and actually it's not as cold and calculating as it might appear. It's more that the old norms of life have long disappeared, and need replacing with something different. Please don't fantasise that life in the past was easier or better than today. Courtship and romance in bygone years were only for the young. If you were widowed or divorced in mid-life, then you had little chance of finding love again, so from that point of view thank your lucky stars! Despite the current fad for women finding Jane Austen novels wonderfully romantic, so that that cold horror of a man Mr Darcy has been put on a global pedestal as the 'most romantic' of mankind, the truth was that young women were desperate to be married off, as they had no money or chance of a life at all without a husband, and were a drain on their fathers' resources while they remained unmarried. None of us know what actually happened once the golden couple crossed the horizon into marriage. Mr Darcy might have galloped as quickly back to London and left poor Elizabeth on her own in draughty Pemberley. She would have had little recourse for alternative action. We have far more freedom today, and the ability to bring about change in our lives. But freedom, choice and change come with a price tag. That's what you're going to learn about in this book. How to handle the price – and get your money's worth!

Maybe it's time for a 'dating detox'

One way to solve the problem is to think about a period of 'dating detox' before you set that toe in the murky waters. The stigma of what used to be known as 'lonely hearts', whereby any man or woman who advertised in the personal columns or signed up to an agency was seen as sad, or a failure, or even pathetic, has long gone. Dating is so widespread. The internet has opened up totally new avenues and made it all more 'normal' and even 'natural'. None of us need feel the slightest twinge of guilt or shame to be heart-on-sleeve dating. Yet I suspect that most of us – when we face up to the fact we've been spending too many evenings in front of the TV, or with the same group of friends, acting desperately jolly out on the town, when all we really want is to find someone to share our lives with – still have to swallow a fair amount of pride – 'This shouldn't be happening to me, surely I can meet a partner in the normal social round?'

●●●●●●●●●●●

'I found going out a lot of hard work.'

Here is Jason, 28, from Leeds who often found himself spending time away in other cities for his job. Jason is one of the first to admit that when he initially tried internet dating, the very thought of it made him nervous and rather embarrassed.

I was often away for a few weeks at a time, living in another town, in hotels or rented flats. I was becoming increasingly frustrated that the only way to meet girls was to go out drinking with my mates. It didn't seem a likely way to meet someone special. I lived on my own in a flat in Leeds but the rent was expensive, and suddenly I was finding myself very much on my own.

Before that, after being a student, I'd always been able to share houses with friends. But they'd begun to pair up and settle down. So what was I to do? When you're in your early 20s, you're not even thinking of finding a partner or having a relationship, though I had lived with a couple of girlfriends. I would go out drinking with my mates on Friday nights. On Saturdays, we'd play football and then be out drinking again in the evening. Sundays were spent slouching on the sofa in front of the TV. In all honesty, I think I found going out a lot of hard work. I can't think of anyone I know who met someone serious on a night out drinking. My other mates who have wives or partners either met them as students or have got together with old friends. I'd had this secret thought that there might be someone living round the corner who I might never meet!

On a whim he tried the Dating Direct site, and instantly came across Sally's profile. He sent her a jokey email: 'I didn't want to sound like a loser. It's male pride I suppose.'

At the time, I was away in Edinburgh for two to three weeks before we could even meet for our first date. What I found was ironically the internet gave me the opportunity to meet someone naturally. You can get to know someone, without having to meet first, with all the social pressure that brings. I've been on some first dates that were really terrible. You've no idea who you're with or why. Yet, within a couple of months, I knew Sally was the girl I wanted to marry.

Sally was only 22 when she first started going online with www.DatingDirect.com. Yet she says she had already become sick of going out with guys that messed her around or were cheating.

I'd got into a rut of really bad self-esteem and wanted to try to feel better about myself. I went speed dating once with a group of girlfriends, but it all seemed so cold. I couldn't imagine really meeting anyone that way.

When Jason first made contact online, he was in Edinburgh and we couldn't meet up for three weeks. We talked on the phone and emailed each other a lot. I was still quite nervous of meeting anyone. Then on Valentine's Day he sent me an e-card. I knew he was going to be back in Leeds soon, so we just waited and talked a lot on the phone. He sounded so nice, I began to let myself believe he might be a genuinely nice guy.

When we did meet, it was so easy, as though we knew each other, because we'd already found out so much background. We went for a meal and to the cinema. He immediately asked to see me again and booked tickets for the rugby. We began seeing each other every two or three evenings. It progressed quickly when he moved back to Leeds. After six or eight weeks, he moved in with me. At the time I was living at my mum's, as she needed the rent, and we all got on really well. I think she liked having a young man about the house to help out. One of the things I like about how we met is that we could possibly have met in the past. He goes to the same gym as my brother. There does seem to be a bit of fate in it all.

In that story of Jason and Sally, two perfectly normal young people, you might have noticed how he describes the shallow emptiness of that 'blokey' way of socialising, based around drinking with the lads and barely meeting young women. Also Sally spoke of her battered self-esteem from being messed about by other young guys. These two didn't need too much detoxing as things sorted themselves out very easily for them. But if you've been finding yourself remaining single for just that little bit too long, then it's time to start looking deeply into yourself and working on both your inner and outer self-image.

• • • • • • • • • • •

Some reasons you may be single

I don't want to imply you've maybe got a serious problem that could land you in prison. I doubt you're psychotic or sociopathic. It's more likely that you've allowed one or two very basic fears and foibles to take too strong a hold. Here's a list I've compiled of reasons we might hide in front of the TV rather than get ourselves out there looking:

- *You think you're not sufficiently good-looking – too fat, too thin, too tall/short, not enough hair, complexion not perfect. First, you want to get your looks in order, then you'll worry about dating.*

It's true that men are more influenced by looks. But, if you feel you don't come over most attractive on a photo basis, then try other forms of dating, whereby you meet face-to-face first. Looks are really not only skin deep. The major part of how we come across to others is to do with how we feel about ourselves and project that feeling. We must all know friends who seem to attract men/women without any effort, yet they're not really any better looking than the rest of us.

- *You've got to get your flat fixed up, your job/career sorted, wait for your mother to get well, wait till the dog has died.*

  It's true that there are times in life when we are just not ready for love, or romance, or maybe anything much more than the company of old and close friends. If there are these huge hurdles in your life right now and you feel that you would not be interesting or exciting company for a potential date, than maybe this is the time to sit out the next dance. But don't just sit there moping. Use this opportunity to work on your appearance, clothes, positive lifestyle. Get out to the gym, make sure you walk a lot more, join a few outside networking groups or take up new hobbies. Focus on improving your life all round, so when the major obstacles have moved on, you'll be ready for another change in your life.

- *Every time you meet someone new, you end up feeling more desolate and alone afterwards, so you feel it's just not worth the effort. Maybe you're better off on your own after all?*

The problem you're expressing here is very common. The fear is of rejection and abandonment. Opening ourselves up to new people, and to the potential of being loved or finding someone we can love too, can be terrifying, as it reawakens probable childhood panics of being deserted, by mother or father, and the inevitable alarm that arouses. If this fear of rejection is a very powerful emotion for you, it might be worthwhile seeking some counselling or psychotherapy to try to come to terms with it first. Going out on a date does not mean you will be abandoned, or that if you offer love it will be rejected. Going out on a date just possibly means you might meet someone whose company you enjoy or who will offer you new friendship. Rejection when someone doesn't want to see you again need be no more heartbreaking than you would expect someone to feel if you turned them down. You have to develop a reasonably thick skin. You've been for job interviews, haven't you, that didn't work out? Did you mope about that experience for long too? Remember it's all quite normal and natural.

- *Your job is so time-consuming, so all-embracing, that you just don't have time to give to someone else. Dating doesn't work for you because men or women who you meet soon turn off when you can't make yourself free or available to go to a film or even meet for dinner.*

If this is genuinely the reason that you keep out of the dating scene, then you might have to seriously consider the role your career is playing in your life. Do you want to end up married to the job? I know that these days employers expect their pound of flesh, if not ounce of blood, particularly if you are high-powered and a high earner. But will the smart apartment, the posh car, and an empty life really satisfy you for many years to come? Take some practical steps. In your case, the internet can be the best way to at least get to know new people online. If you are honest about your time commitments, you might find a compatible partner in a similar line of work. Try to devote weekends to dating, and turn off the Blackberry or mobile so that you can't be called into the office. Maybe a singles holiday would be good experience for you, where you have a few days to meet people. Or, if you are genuinely earning enough, then a personalised introduction agency would be best able to find you a suitable partner.

- *You're only just getting over a broken heart, even though it's been a year or so since that relationship broke up. You're not ready to go back out into the dating arena.*

A broken heart is not the best ground on which to build a new relationship. But even if you're not really ready for the next full-on relationship, that should not prevent you from dating. Remember when you were at school, all the boys and girls in the playground eyeing each other up and working out who fancied whom? That's what dating should emulate. It's not a desperate 'I must have a permanent partner in my life' world, but more a casual 'let's see if we can be friends even, if not lovers' arena. There are a lot of men and women out there who are looking for flirtation, romance, sex – and not permanence – and that kind of dating might suit you at this time. Broken hearts heal with time. Well, they do if you let them. However, if you nurse the broken heart, as though it were a baby bird that needs to be suckled to be kept alive, it will hold you back forever.

Sometimes rushing into a fling can help tide you over and even boost your flagging self-confidence, if a broken relationship has left you with a large attack of angst about yourself. But beware the first relationship in such a situation. Very often you'll find yourself latching on to somebody, maybe just for the sake of 'finding someone in your life'.

- *You know what you want. You have a very strong picture in your mind's eye of the man or woman you want to meet, with whom you'll be happy. But you just don't get to meet that type of person, so you've decided to give up the dating game. It's not worth the misery!*

Could it be that your expectations are too high? I don't mean that you should be prepared to pair yourself off with the next available person. But it might be that you're adopting the 'checklist' attitude to dating. Many men complain that women seem to have incredibly high expectations and that they'll just write off a man who doesn't meet their criteria: looks – he must be stunning; earning power – got to be higher than hers; car – forget any rust under the bonnet; holidays – woo me with romance and adventure;

manners – must know how to get a table at a good restaurant and understand wines, etc, etc. The truth is that these women are creating a stick with which to beat their own backs. Men can sense when you're checking off the tick boxes. You have to try to show some flexibility, and open yourself up for change.

One woman I met, who was recently divorced and in her mid-50s, confessed that she didn't have a clue about dating, as she'd been with her husband since her early-20s. 'But I know what I'm looking for,' she said over-confidently. 'He must love opera, run his own business, be sophisticated and well-travelled.' Ouch. I wanted to say: 'Good luck, but maybe try to open yourself up to the idea of meeting someone slightly different?' I just got the feeling her intransigence wasn't going to lead to great success.

•••••••••••

'A lot of women seem to think they'll find a Mr Darcy.'

Chris, who we met briefly in Chapter 1, has some views about women's often overly high expectations:

A lot of women seem to think they'll find a Mr Darcy who will turn up and sweep them off their feet. They've got a preconceived notion of what would be the perfect match for them. Often it's a case of wanting to find all the things that were missing in their marriage or previous relationships. Many of the women I meet are considerably better off than me in terms of equity at least, but they still expect men to have as much money as they do. What do men fantasise finding? Something similar I suppose, really hot and passionate, yet meaningful. That's partly why a lot of men look for younger women – not only are they the 'trophy' partner to have on your arm, but they might come with less baggage.

• • • • • • • • • • •

- *You're worried that potential dates find you desperate – that's the comment you hear back, if you get any feedback at all.*

Desperation is the worst card to play if you're going on a new date. No one wants to feel that they are going to be the answer to someone else's total-life problems. Be very careful not to top-load your conversation with misery, gloom or instantly planning a future together.

Women can be too free with their critical judgement of other men, along the lines of the 'all men are bastards' critique. If you are really looking for marriage and babies, then it's best to either sign up to a serious online dating site, or join a personal introduction agency, so that you are honest about those expectations. But be careful that you don't let that need become one that's all-embracing. One man I spoke to described how he sometimes felt like a potential 'sperm donor', as all the women in their mid- to late-30s were eyeing him up as the potential father to their children.

Not only women come over as desperate. Men can be just as bad at moaning about their ex-wives, then trying to find the next woman to fit her into the slot left by their former wife. The following story by Annie tells something of that tale.

• • • • • • • • • • •

'Men have proposed marriage within a week or so of meeting!'

Annie, who was 51 when she first started dating again five years ago, has a remarkably healthy attitude to dating despite some varied experiences. She split up with her husband of 25 years, and with two grown daughters and an interesting career, she is smartly dressed and a sharp thinker. In these years, she's had a few quite long-lasting relationships, and, amazingly, is still quite happy about the situation as well as being thoughtful about the 'emotional baggage' problem, on both sides, and what are realistic expectations:

At first, I found that I still had some emotional baggage from my marriage, but the men have tons of baggage too. They often seem ready to rush into relationships. They just want something to be there. They can be clingy with you all the time. They think they're ready for a relationship, but they're not. I've met men who have proposed marriage within a week or so of meeting! Or they want to move in with me. The big 'c' [commitment] word crowds the picture. It can be a real minefield. There's a pushiness, a rush to 'get out there', but no one really knows where.

When I first started dating at just over 50, I was really suffering from the idea a woman my age wouldn't be attractive to men. But I've learnt how wrong that attitude can be! I've probably met about 30 or so men. It's been fun. I love meeting new people, even if I'm not really attracted to them.

• • • • • • • • • •

Having read my pointers for reasons that may be holding you back on the dating scene, why not take this quiz to see if you are the kind of person who makes their own luck. After all, that's what it mostly comes down to.

Quiz

Are you lucky in love or do you make your own luck?

1. *You are going on a hot date with someone for the first time. It was arranged three days beforehand and you're going out for dinner. What's your attitude to the date?*

   a) I'll just be completely myself. If he/she doesn't fancy me then it wasn't meant to be anyway.

   b) I'll do everything I can think of to maximise the

chances of getting a second date. This would include planning what I'm going to wear, making sure it's clean and ironed, having a shower beforehand and getting ready so I look my best, and making a big effort to be good company on the date.

c) I'll make sure I turn up on time and look nice, but making too much effort seems a bit desperate.

d) I'll make a reasonable effort, but I don't think I'd put myself out completely as it's not going to make a huge difference. I can only be myself.

2. *If all goes well on the date and you fancy him/her, in general what would you say your chances are of him/her wanting to go on another date with you?*

a) Very unlikely, people generally don't find me attractive.

b) Unlikely; it's possible, but I'm probably an acquired taste.

c) About a 50–50 chance.

d) A good chance. If there's chemistry there then it's likely to be a two-way thing.

e) Very likely. If I fancy him/her, I'll have made a big effort, which will hopefully pay off.

3. *If you're single, why are you still single? (If you're not single, try to remember the reasons when you were last single.)*

a) I haven't been on a date in ages – I just haven't been lucky enough to meet the right person.

b) I've been very busy with other things and I haven't

had enough time to put into meeting someone or developing a relationship.

c) I've only been single for a short time but I'm confident I'll meet someone new when I feel ready.

d) I'm very fussy and the right person hasn't come along.

e) It's just fate. I'm obviously meant to be on my own for the time being.

f) I'm definitely not interested in a relationship right now.

4. *If you were to make a bigger effort with your appearance so you really looked your best, do you think it could have any effect on meeting a new partner?*

a) Yes. I think more people would find me attractive, either because of my improved appearance or increased confidence and it would increase the chances of attracting the right person.

b) Yes. I think more people would be attracted to me and this could increase the chances of getting to know someone who could be right for me.

c) Very unsure. It might work, but I'm not convinced it would make a huge difference.

d) I don't think it would make much difference – it's either going to happen or it's not. Someone doesn't ask you out on a date because you've had a new haircut.

e) If someone's right for you and you're meant to be together, then something like that doesn't matter.

5. *If you had to make a guess, what would you say are your chances of ever meeting someone who you will have a lifelong relationship with?*

   a) A very good chance. It's just a matter of finding the person you're meant to be with.

   b) A very good chance as it's what most people aspire to, but it's about meeting people and then putting in the effort to sustain a relationship when you've met someone.

   c) It's possible, but I don't think it's something that I have much control over.

   d) Unlikely. Few people are lucky enough to meet the right person.

   e) It's possible, but it's down to a combination of meeting the right person, putting in the effort and other factors outside my control.

6. *Which of the following do you believe has the biggest influence over whether you'll meet someone who you'll fall in love with and have a long-term relationship with?*

   a) Fate.

   b) Destiny.

   c) Luck.

   d) Random chance encounters.

   e) Making an effort to meet new people.

   f) Starting up conversations with more people.

   g) Using internet dating.

7. *If you're out in a bar, do you think that approaching people you find attractive increases the chances of meeting someone who could be right for you?*
   a) Yes. The more people you meet the more likely it is that you'll meet the right person.
   b) Yes, it would probably increase the odds somewhat, but there's still a significant element of chance.
   c) It would just mean more rejections or more one-night stands or more casual flings. You're either going to meet the right person at any given time or you're not.
   d) You can't just make the right person materialise. It's more to do with fate.

8. *Imagine you've been seeing someone new for four weeks. You've seen each other about three times a week, it's going well and it's starting to feel like you're boyfriend and girlfriend. How much effort would you still be making with him/her?*
   a) I'd be making a big effort at this stage. I'd try and look my best and be good company and always tidy up properly when he/she came round to my place. I'd be suggesting we went out on dates together rather than sitting in watching TV.
   b) I'd be making an effort, but I'd probably relax a bit by this stage. I'd want him/her to see how I live my life.
   c) I'd make the effort to go out on a date now and then and mostly have a shower before we met up, but by now it would be very relaxed.

d) I'd want him/her to see me completely as I am. It shouldn't be about what I look like or how tidy my place is. If he/she doesn't like me the way I am then we're not right for each other anyway.

9. *Say you've been together for at least a year, does the effort you put into sustaining a relationship at this stage (making an effort to listen to your partner, making time for each other, surprising your partner, still going on dates) make any difference to the success of the relationship?*
a) No. If you've been lucky enough to find your perfect partner, then it shouldn't be an effort.
b) No. It's either going to work out or it's not. Bending over backwards to please someone just prolongs the agony.
c) It might help things if it's borderline anyway, but ultimately it probably doesn't make any difference as to whether you'll stay together for ever.
d) Yes. It might not be the only factor, but it will definitely help.
e) Yes. I think a large part of the success of a relationship is a direct consequence of my actions.

Your answers

1. a) 0 b) 4 c) 2 d) 1
2. a) 0 b) 1 c) 2 d) 3 e) 4
3. a) 0 b) 3 c) 4 d) 1 e) 0 f) 3
4. a) 4 b) 3 c) 2 d) 1 e) 0

5. a) 2 b) 4 c) 0 d) 0 e) 3
6. a) 0 b) 0 c) 0 d) 1 e) 4 f) 3 g) 3
7. a) 4 b) 3 c) 1 d) 0
8. a) 4 b) 3 c) 1 d) 0
9. a) 0 b) 0 c) 1 d) 3 e) 4

Scoring

You're a mover and a shaker – you make your own luck (30–36)

You're a confident person and probably successful in most areas of your life. Your success may be due to the belief that what happens is down to your own actions, or it may be that you've acquired this belief through your success. Either way, your belief that you're in control of your life and your own destiny is one that many high achievers share. Of course, it's sometimes worth remembering that we're all human and you don't have to achieve perfection all of the time (even if you'll always aim for it). Keep making the effort but if things don't go how you'd like in a relationship, try not to be too hard on yourself. It takes two to tango after all – it takes two people to make a relationship flourish.

You might make the effort – if you feel it's worth it (12–29)

You do accept that making an effort to meet people and making an effort once you're in a relationship are important. However, sometimes you just pay lip service to this. You do recognise that you'll have to make a bit of an effort on a first date, for example. You do have certain standards and you don't want to look like a slob, but you're not convinced that it really makes that much difference in the end.

You're probably more realistic and down-to-earth than the people who feel they can and should control what happens in a relationship; you recognise that there will always be things that are outside your control. Even so, don't be afraid to do everything you need to do to meet the right person. Otherwise you could be letting opportunities pass you by.

You don't feel you have much control over your love life (0–11)
You like to call it fate, luck or destiny. Is this just an excuse for your singledom? Sometimes you might need to give fate a helping hand if you want to see results. People who are successful high-flyers tend to have a strong belief that their life is in their own hands. Perhaps you should consider taking a leaf out of their books and try being a bit more proactive in your search for a partner, if you're really serious about meeting someone.

Some people are too shy for their own good

Now it's time to deal with the one major issue that crops up in so much discussion of dating and whether it will work for you or not. There are those (lucky) people who are genuinely outgoing, who are stimulated by meeting new people, who don't find going into bars or clubs sufficient to induce terminal paranoia, for whom the dating game is maybe easy. Then there are the others. I can guarantee the numbers of people who would classify themselves as 'shy' outnumbers the outgoing, happy-go-lucky ones. If we dig deep, many of us who might come across as quite self-confident or outgoing, would say in private that we are shy. Take us out of our normal comfort zone, work, family, small group of friends, and we feel paralysed by shyness. That's OK. What is not all right is if we let that fear of meeting new people or strangers dominate our lives.

Crippling shyness can often affect young men, more than younger women. The outgoing, sassy young women of today make the situation even worse, as they react to the shy young man with ill-concealed boredom. More mature men and women have had plenty of years to adapt to shyness and probably to respect their own inner shy self too. So what do people who are overly shy do to boost themselves onto the dating scene?

First, there are many different types of dating. The internet might, at face value, appear like a good way for a shy person to meet other people. But even though you might begin to communicate through email or even on the phone, there will still be that dreaded moment when you have to meet. You can almost feel her scorn as she walks in the door of the café or bar. You've managed to mask the shyness with bravura online which doesn't match the reality.

Perhaps the internet is not the best way for someone like you to begin meeting potential dates. Because shyness is a real problem, it would be better to try to join lots of groups or networks, and get to know people more slowly. Although the workplace is generally frowned on as a place to meet dates, if a group of colleagues is going to the pub on a Friday evening after work, or to a skating rink, or bowling alley, do join in.

They'll already know that you are shy and will be tolerant. You might just meet a fellow workmate from a different department, and getting to know someone slowly is by far the best policy.

If your shyness is overtaking your life, then making sure you go out and join groups of people is vital in helping to overcome this tendency. Before even thinking about looking for love or romance, it's best to focus on networking groups. These might have been formed to help people in their careers, or for a sport, or special interest such as film, theatre, the arts or even a book-reading group. You need to get used to being out with other people where there is no pressure to form twosomes. How about joining a running club, a swimming team, or the Ramblers' Association for walks across the gorgeous countryside? If you begin to develop more outside interests, then you will also naturally have more to talk about when you do get round to dating.

• • • • • • • • • •

'A lot of women out there are just looking for a good time.'

Tom, a 44-year-old accountant, with a good career as head of finance for a major firm, is an example of someone who finds the whole world of dating inexplicably difficult, but at least he is doing something about the situation. He doesn't come across as terribly shy, but then neither is he an extroverted character. Tom's reasonably attractive, but perhaps he comes across as rather too solid, dependable and serious. Why do I say that? Because even with his high-earning career and decent looks, so far the world of dating has been a resounding flop! For the past two years, he has tried to meet women by visiting online dating sites. He's sent loads of emails, flirts, and added women to his favourites list, but has just had no success. Now he's realised he'll have to try something new, as not once has he been able to set up a real live date, with a real live woman:

> *Maybe I'm not very photogenic? I earn a good salary, enjoy sports, I go scuba diving, play badminton, golf, enjoy going to restaurants and for drinks. I feel I have a reasonable sense of humour. But women just don't seem to be interested in me. I decided to do something about it and have signed up with a personal introduction agency hoping they might be able to put me together with women who are more my type. I'm forcing myself to go out more to singles events, I tried a cookery evening recently. But I think a lot of women out there are just looking for a good time, or for sex, not for a real relationship.*

• • • • • • • • • • •

How to boost your self-confidence

Even if shyness isn't a problem, lack of self-confidence might well be creating as big an obstacle for you when it comes to dating. A lot happens to us in life, and a bad divorce, or cruel break-up from a previous partner, being made redundant at work, or just feeling generally rather low and worthless, can erode what little fragile self-confidence we once had. The trouble with dating is that you are forced into a situation of looking your best, acting in the most positive way you can, all the while mentally comparing yourself with anyone else who might be competition (which could basically be the remaining 50 per cent of the world's population!).

If you are aware that this lack of self-confidence is holding you back, then do take some positive steps to bring change to your inner attitude. There are many self-development courses out there which can help – even if it's as simple as taking up yoga or Pilates, or signing up to learn a language, or take art or drama classes – anything proactive and positive will help kick start a new 'you', with more confidence and assertiveness. I would personally recommend neuro-linguistic programming (NLP), which really had a powerful impact on my outlook many years ago, when I was feeling particularly low. NLP makes you realise how we allow language, just everyday talk and deliberation, to control our thoughts and actions. NLP is also taught in groups, where you learn to act out mental blocks that are holding you back. I won't give it any bigger plug than that, but as soon as you take on board the fact you've been saying to yourself 'I can't do this, because …' it comes as a relief to let go of those self-imposed restrictions.

If you want to bring about change in your life, through dating and hopefully meeting a new partner, then you first have to bring about inner and, to a degree, outer change too.

So make sure you look deep into yourself and think why you might be holding yourself back, then take action. If it means forcing yourself out into company, joining groups or networks, learning to say 'yes' rather than 'no', then make an effort to do so. You have to push yourself, get out of your comfort zone, be more outwardly friendly, smile at strangers, even talk to someone on the Tube or the bus. Do something different to break the mould.

• • • • • • • • • • • •

'You'll never meet a good woman in the local pub.'

Here's Chris again. Outwardly you would not think he suffers from lack of self-confidence in meeting women. But that's because he can still put forward the face of the businessman, who was once happily married with a family. Now that he and his wife have been divorced a few years, he finds his self-confidence has slipped away. He admits to mistakes that men can make when they first hit the dating scene:

As a man, one of the first things you do when you separate from your wife is to say, 'I've got to find someone else and fast.' There seems to be an impulse to fill the gap, and you sort of assume you'll find someone quite easily. Except you don't. You begin to work out you'll never meet a good woman in the local pub. Women have support groups among their friends, men don't. They just swallow their pride and drink more beer. Then you begin to doubt your social skills and ability to date. In my life, I reached a crisis point when I faced up to the fact I had to do something.

If you Google 'improve your dating technique' or 'female seduction' there's all sorts of sites out there promising to help cure you of your poor social skills. You pay up, do their course, but what they are really saying is, 'It all comes down to confidence, so unless you can change from within, nothing will change.'

The majority of men are very confused. Once I'd realised it was time to move on from the pub, and evening classes were also getting me nowhere, I tried various forms of dating and eventually turned to online dating sites. But my overall opinion of this style of dating is that there's no time or depth to it. If you just give someone two or three weeks and then decide they're not good enough, you move on. It all becomes so impersonal.

There's a stage when I just give up and go into hibernation, or as someone said 'into my caveman mould'. If there's nothing out there that interests me or makes sparks fly, then I don't want to keep trying. But after a while of struggling to go to cinema or theatre on my own, I end up going back and looking hopefully on the sites again. Maybe it would be nice for me to have some really good women friends; to talk to, take to the theatre, go to functions with, so that I have a partner of some kind if not of the totally romantic type.

• • • • • • • • • •

Mid-life dating – starting over can be the scariest experience of all

If you've been in the secure world of marriage most of your adult life, as we have already seen from some of the case studies, and you suddenly find yourself single again – well, there's no way around the fact it's going to be scary and panic-inducing to get back out there on the singles scene. By now, easy to network groups such as old school or university friends may have long disappeared. Or, even if you have some contact with them, you may feel too lacking in self-confidence to let them know you're back 'in the market'. There are no easy answers, but you do have to take the plunge.

If you read over the preceding sections about how to help boost your self-confidence, or self-esteem, you'll have taken the first hurdle. Next is trying to find which is the best way to go about dating. If you are a single parent, there are networking groups for similar people. However, the likelihood is you'll find mostly women in these groups, and women in such circumstances can be very competitive about lending out potential male partners. Join groups of any kind, from book-reading groups to politically oriented parties, sports, dance, arts, evening classes, wine-tasting, local walking tours – anything and everything. OK, if you have young children, it will all depend on the amount of free time you can negotiate or barter for. Hopefully, your ex will take his/her turn with the children.

One of the virtues of the online dating world is that sites are created to cover an amazing variety of needs. There are now several such sites for single parents (see back of the book in the Resources section). Single fathers will feature as much as single mothers on such online sites. In your case, having to email a lot first, or make phone contact, can be a lifeline. Need I say this, but be very careful about rushing headlong into the next full-blown relationship. An angry single parent who feels used and abused by a former partner is not going to be in the best frame of mind to start out on a new relationship right now. Be careful too about jumping into bed with the first person to turn up. You may be feeling starved of love and affection, but you will have to learn to adapt to the changing world of dating these days. There is a lot of sexual activity out there that is never going to lead to a real relationship. You don't want to get hurt all over again.

Having said that, flexibility and a willingness to see a relationship outside of the norm you were used to will be your best lines of action. The world has changed, you have to adapt and learn to enjoy its differences. Whatever you do, don't feel that just because you have children, you are therefore unlovable. The likelihood is that there is a full-time, or part-time, single parent just waiting to meet someone like you.

In some ways, it can be even harder if you are a mid-lifer, newly single again, without children. Why? Because there may be an inner, unresolved, sadness at your childlessness which, as a woman, once you have passed say 45 or 50 years, you won't be able to do anything about. Men at a similar age of course can continue to father children, but do they really want to? So many unanswered questions in this age group can make finding a new partner rather difficult. As Chris again has said about men in his age range, 'There's no role model for what age 45-plus living should be like. I see people on these TV programmes buying properties abroad, couples doing exciting new things together, but the reality is a lot of people living on their own and feeling miserable.'

• • • • • • • • • • •

'Something electric blew up between us.'

Lesley is an actress in her 50s, who, after 23 years of marriage, has been divorced for five years and still finds dating and meeting potential partners strangely unreal and decidedly uncomfortable. She reflects misgivings shared by others, though not everyone feels this so strongly:

> *I'd been married for so long, it was as if we'd grown up together. We met as drama students and it was a helluva shock, after over 20 years together, when he announced one day he was no longer in love with me and was leaving. I just hadn't seen it coming. The other problem, I suppose, was that I'd lived a lot in his shadow and had allowed his career to take precedence over mine. However, my enforced freedom made me concentrate on getting my working life back together, and I am passionate about what I do now. But, ten years down the line from his leaving, it still hurts like hell.*
>
> *I moved back to London. I've always been in the freelance*

world, but I'd forgotten how hard it would be at first to build up a social life again. I never had children, and thought I had lots of friends and contacts through work, but that doesn't really pan out when you're suddenly single and back on the scene.

But at the time, I was energised and made a lot of effort. However, my friends were either in cosy marriages or single women like me, or gay male pals. I went on one of those group holidays for singles where there were only two men to 20 women. I did well and slept with one of the men. That did a lot for my self-confidence. It was great to have a holiday romance! But he was an IT nerd, quite withdrawn and rather socially inept, and we really had nothing in common. After that, I began to think seriously about trying out internet dating. I just had to find ways to meet more men.

I signed up to www.loveandfriends.co.uk as their members looked closest to my type. I began dating one of them, who lived hundreds of miles away, and again we had nothing in common. One evening, however, something strange happened. I hadn't been that keen on him, seeing him more as a friend, when something electric blew up between us. We had a mad few weeks, when we were really passionate about each other. We'd write our life stories to each other on email. We were developing a relationship through the written word. He could be incredibly romantic on email.

We agreed to go away together for a few days and stayed on a nice farm in the country. You wouldn't believe it – all the romance just vanished when we were together. We spent four nights in the same bed, but nothing happened. That was it. He'd dropped from the ether into my life, and six weeks later had vanished as quickly.

• • • • • • • • • • •

But then for others in mid-life, even with children, pets, ex-wives and lovers, success can also just be around the corner. Sometimes, it might come down to having a strong sense of what went wrong before and knowing not to make the same mistakes again. People who really want a relationship, who are prepared to be flexible and let someone into their lives, often do find what they are looking for.

• • • • • • • • • • •

'He seemed so funny and down-to-earth.'

David and Patricia are in their mid-40s. David started dating a couple of years ago, after separating from his wife of seven years. Their seven-year-old daughter stays with him a couple of nights a week and some weekends. Patricia, at 42, had newly emerged from a seven-year relationship and she has two children aged seven and nine. Both David and Patricia remember separately reading an article about internet dating and some success stories. They both knew they were looking for a similarly serious-minded person with integrity. David works in IT as an engineer, and the chances for him of meeting women through work are slim. Patricia's work is in the rehabilitation of people with brain injuries. She's no extrovert and was unlikely to go into bars or pubs.

Patricia: *I'd been on four or five dates with other men, then I came across David. He seemed so down-to-earth and funny. He wrote about himself that he's house-trained and his username was 'bloke on a bike'.*

David: *It was Patricia's photo that struck me. We swapped emails and chatted on the phone one evening. She was interesting, not just your average run-of-the-mill woman. I'd put a lot of work and thought into my profile, to show myself in the best light, trying to sound light and humorous. What's funny is that although we lived in different northern cities, our paths could have crossed many times, as I was a student 20 years ago in the town she lives in. We used to drink at the same places, and we both like walking, climbing, food, drinking and music.*

Patricia: *I wish I'd met David years ago, but on the other hand we probably appreciate each other more as things haven't worked out for either of us in the past. I set out with the deliberate aim to find someone the opposite of my previous partner. I wanted to be with someone who I have a lot of respect for, can laugh with and enjoy doing social and leisure activities together.*

We decided to move in together quite quickly, maybe as we're both a bit older you begin to realise time might be short. Our kids are of similar ages, and even though we had a few settling-in problems, the two girls who are in the same class at school are like sisters now. I have a cat and a dog – his daughter loves the cat and David seems to have bonded with my smelly dog.

● ● ● ● ● ● ● ● ● ●

So now you've absorbed all this information, why not take another of our friendly quizzes, to see if you've got yourself sorted?

Quiz

Are you really ready to settle down?

Are you the marrying type – can't wait to get hitched? Or would the mere thought of it make you run a mile? You may think you know the answer already, but take this quick and easy test to find out if you're as ready to settle down as you think you are, or whether you're more of a commitment-phobe.

1. *Why are you still single? Try to choose the answer that most applies to you.*

   a) I'm too busy at work to socialise much.

   b) I don't know why, I just haven't met the right person yet.

   c) I'd like to meet someone but I'm quite shy at approaching men/women.

   d) Meeting someone just isn't a priority for me at the moment as my life is full in other ways.

   e) I've been hurt in the past and I don't think I'd trust anyone at the moment.

2. *Imagine you meet the love of your life, the person you could imagine spending the rest of your life with. Would you be willing to make any changes to your work for the benefit of the relationship?*
   a) I'd be willing to be more organised and self-disciplined at work so that I could leave at a decent time.
   b) I'd be happy to go in earlier and leave work earlier.
   c) My career is important to me and I don't think any changes would be necessary or desirable.
   d) I'd never make any sacrifices in my career for a man/woman.
   e) I'd be willing to find a different job, provided it was a suitable job, so we could be together.
   f) I can't wait to meet the love of my life, get married, give up work and have kids.

3. *Imagine you've met a fantastic man/woman. You decide to live together for the first time. If things were going really well, would you move to another area that would be more practical for both of you, for example, for travelling to work?*
   a) Yes, I don't see why not.
   b) Yes, but only if it was really necessary.
   c) Unlikely.
   d) No. I like my home and I'm settled in this area so I wouldn't consider it.
   e) No. He/she could move into my place as I wouldn't consider moving.

4. *If you moved in with someone or got married, do you think you'd go out with your friends less than when you were single?*
   a) I'd still make an effort to see my friends, but I think it's inevitable that I'd see a bit less of them.
   b) I'd probably try to see them even more, just to prove a point.
   c) I'd go out even more because I'd have more spare cash once my living expenses were shared.
   d) I don't think it would make any difference. I wouldn't become the sort of person who puts a relationship before their friends.

5. *Imagine you were to live with someone, what are your first thoughts about the day-to-day practicalities of sharing your life with someone?*
   a) What a nightmare. I'm used to my single, independent way of life.
   b) We'd need to get a cleaner.
   c) It would be lovely sharing my life with someone special.
   d) I'm used to doing what I want, when I want. I think I'd find it hard to adapt, but hopefully it would be worth it.
   e) I think there would be things that would irritate me, but that's life. I'm sure that with the right person the benefits would outweigh the minor irritations.

6. *Could you see yourself getting married?*
   a) No. I can't see that happening.
   b) Maybe, but unlikely.
   c) Perhaps one day.
   d) It's a big commitment that scares me. Maybe I'd feel differently if I met the right person.
   e) I'd like to get married one day.
   f) It's what I want in the future. I'm just looking for Mr/Miss Right so I can settle down into wedded bliss.

7. *How do you feel about being faithful to one person in a long-term relationship?*
   a) I've been unfaithful in the past and I think realistically I'd be tempted to stray again.
   b) I'm not ready for a serious monogamous relationship. Just now I'm more interested in having fun.
   c) It's the ideal to aim for, but I'm not sure it's possible.
   d) Trust and fidelity are very important to me and would be essential in a long-term relationship.

8. *Is it possible to find the perfect partner?*
   a) Yes, I think there's someone perfect for me out there somewhere.
   b) Not sure. I like to think it is.
   c) I think it should be possible to find someone I'm really compatible with, but there's no such thing as perfection.

d) I don't know and at the moment I don't care.

e) No. The majority of relationships break down sooner or later and people who do stay together for ever are just settling rather than remaining truly happy.

9. *Is it desirable to spend your life with one person?*

a) No. I don't think we're genetically designed to mate for life.

b) No. I can't say that it's something I desperately aspire to.

c) I'm not sure at the moment.

d) Ideally yes, but life's not always like that in reality.

e) Yes. This is what I'd be looking for when I meet the right man/woman.

Your answers

1. a) 1 b) 0 c) 0 d) 4 e) 3
2. a) 1 b) 1 c) 3 d) 4 e) 0 f) 0
3. a) 0 b) 1 c) 2 d) 4 e) 3
4. a) 0 b) 4 c) 4 d) 2
5. a) 4 b) 1 c) 0 d) 2 e) 1
6. a) 4 b) 3 c) 2 d) 3 e) 1 f) 0
7. a) 3 b) 4 c) 2 d) 0
8. a) 0 b) 1 c) 1 d) 4 e) 3
9. a) 4 b) 3 c) 2 d) 1 e) 0

Scoring

Get me to the church on time (0–4)

You can't wait to meet the love of your life, settle down for ever and live happily ever after. Good luck to you: I hope you find your match. You tend to be trusting and optimistic, which can have advantages and disadvantages. Just be careful that you don't see settling down as an alternative to achieving what you want to in life. Most people would ideally like to find a fulfilling long-term relationship, but watch out that you're not expecting complete perfection in a partner or in a relationship, as it just isn't realistic. And when you do meet the love of your life, aim to achieve a balance with other areas of your life, as this will make for a healthier relationship in the long run.

Feet on the ground, but still fit to commit (5–10)

You seem to have struck the right balance between wanting a committed relationship and also wanting to be fulfilled in other areas of your life. Your answers indicate a healthy and mature attitude. You recognise that nobody is perfect, yourself included, and that relationships require effort and the occasional sacrifice in order to make things work.

Provided you are meeting people and dating now and then, you probably won't stay single for too long. Your natural tendency is to want to be in a relationship, and while you recognise a commitment as something serious, any problems that arise will not be because of any abnormal fear of commitment on your part.

Maybe one day (in a galaxy far, far away) (11–27)

You're not completely averse to the idea of a serious long-term committed relationship, but it doesn't seem that it's something you aspire to at the moment. You're just too busy with your work and social life, or perhaps you're just more of an independent free spirit.

If you do decide that you're looking for a spot of long-term monogamy after all, you may need to consider changing your ways. Unless you find someone who's almost identical to you, you might want to think about the concepts of flexibility and compromise. Making big sacrifices could be a step too far for you right now, but some degree of compromise will always be necessary in a relationship.

Commitment-phobe (aka emotionally unavailable) (28–36)

Perhaps you're newly single for the first time in a while, or perhaps you're just young and enjoying sewing your wild oats for the time being. Either way, you're really not looking for any form of serious relationship right now. Have fun and enjoy yourself. It only really becomes a problem if your avoidance of commitment is causing distress to yourself or others.

Chapter 3

Is it Time to Give Online Dating a Try?

Unless you've been happily tucked away in a secure marriage or partnership for the past few years, or on Mars, you've most likely already looked into some online dating sites, or know friends and colleagues who are active users. The growth of internet dating, as it tends to be called, has been nothing short of phenomenal in the past five to six years.

There are more than 100 independent online dating agencies in the United Kingdom, and some say the figure worldwide is in the thousands. The pool of potential partners is enormous. The freedom to search for suitable people, browse profiles, look at photos, make contact, chat on email, by text or phone, arrange to meet, is unprecedented. Maybe it was a freedom experienced in former more polite days, when match-makers made arrangements for young men to view and choose between suitable young women. But that was only for one age group and class: those looking to marry, bear children, and bring their property portfolios together in legal wedlock.

Online is now the most popular way to meet someone not only in the United Kingdom, but across Europe, Australia, the United States and China. Not to discount the other methods of dating, the all-new wholesome truth is that you are more likely to meet someone through some form of dating service than in a bar or in the workplace. A recent survey (by internet dating company Parship) came up with these figures:

- 65 per cent of singles said they had used some form of free or paid for online dating service.
- 24 per cent had been on a blind date arranged by friends.
- 13 per cent used a traditional introduction or matchmaking agency.
- 3 per cent went speed dating.
- 5 per cent had been to singles clubs and 2 per cent on singles holidays.
- 18 per cent placed or responded to a personal ad in a newspaper.
- 50 per cent of singles expect to meet someone through an internet dating service, compared with 18 per cent who say they'll never go online to find love.

The online forum, whether that means social networking sites such as MySpace, Bebo, Facebook, or specific internet dating sites, is now so common that it has just about lost any of the old stigma – the 'you only meet serious weirdos on such sites' comments from friends, family or colleagues. Whether it is now universally accepted as the best thing since that old piece of sliced bread, however, is a question that has still not yet been finally answered.

In its defence, or in hyping up its PR potential, all sorts of pundits have produced their beliefs about why. I've talked before about the fact that people feel more isolated these days, and why finding a partner or mate can become increasingly difficult once the days of school, college or university are way behind us. For today's singles, particularly those in professional careers (for whom the use of the internet and computers is second nature, finding a mate through the internet often makes sense.

The process offers the possibility of being more in control of your destiny, and enables you to connect with like-minded people at home or anywhere around the world. It has a distinctly 21st-century feel to it. The rationale is that courting or meeting a potential partner online comes naturally to the human brain, more so than hooking up through a chance encounter in a pub or bar. It harks back to the days when match-makers or parents would try to fix us up with someone from the next village or tribe. You would know something about this person beforehand. You might have been shown a picture (even a painting, before photography) and your family would have talked about his/her personality or virtues.

Cor blimey, this must be all right then. Yes?

Well, the answer is a decided 'maybe'. The rotten sad truth is that for some it works wonders. For others, it's more like a foot in the door to a new kind of addiction – offering the lure of 'false hope'.

• • • • • • • • • • •

'In poker too, you're convinced tonight this is the one.'

Lenny, a musician, 34, tall, good-looking, says he loves being single, and as someone who also indulges in online gambling, maybe he sums it up for everyone. It's a little like the lottery: you've got to be in it to win it. But, holding out for hope against unrealistic expectations of a 'win' is probably foolish:

> *I've looked into online sites as, generally speaking, I'm up for all new experiences. I also go online to play poker and came up with this interesting connection between gambling and dating. In poker, you get given a pair of cards and you invest all your worldly hopes in that 'pair'. You're convinced tonight this is the one. Then you end up losing a lot of money!*

'I had lots of fun outings.'

Or here is Carrie, who lives in Australia and became involved in online dating while back in the United Kingdom for a year, by then in her mid-50s. Carrie is very attractive and fun-loving. In the photo on her profile, she was standing proudly in front of her fairly old, but much-loved, sports car. In real life, she'd come out of a bad marriage, then thought she'd found the love of her life in an old university friend, who rather quickly ended their relationship after six months:

It was the summer, three years ago. I'd just been dumped and was feeling pretty low. I simply thought, why not give it a try. I didn't know that many people in England and certainly no single men. I have to say that over the next six months or so my experiences were more positive than negative. I met several interesting men and was wined and dined – and occasionally bedded – and altogether given a Good Time. I had a trip to Paris, tickets to a Patti Smith concert, weekends in Hastings and lots of fun outings. On the down side, I did occasionally meet a total dud.

Of course, in the end, there was no one really special. I came to the conclusion that if I don't meet someone in the natural course of my life, then so be it. I won't try the totally artificial websites again.

Asked whether, when she returned to Australia, she went back online, Carrie said:

No, Australia is too small, with none of the safe anonymity of the UK. Also, I have never (well, only once) been attracted to Australian men. I came to the conclusion the whole thing is artificial because there you all are, putting the best possible spin on yourself to a cyberspace full of strangers, and of course we all have warts. Plus, until you actually meet someone and observe their behaviour, listen to their speech, watch how they carry themselves, how can you possibly know whether or not you'll find them attractive? And at our age, we all carry so much baggage we need porters!

• • • • • • • • • • •

Getting internet savvy

Before embarking on the journey through the sometimes murky waters of internet dating sites, please get street-smart and realise that there are several different types of internet sites. Make sure you choose the type of site that best suits your needs, finances or time constraints.

- The 'free' online sites offer a wide variety of names and photos, and you are left to pre-select and make the first contact. The sites are paid for by advertising and click technology. Despite the myth of the internet offering services for free (and many seemingly sensible people have said to me they wouldn't pay for an internet dating site, as you can get all the same information for free), I presume we've more or less woken up to the old adage that there is no such thing as 'free' in this world. You might be able to access hundreds of likely people, but there has been no pre-screening, no financial check on even their credit card details, let alone the truth in what they have written about themselves, or even their photo. You do the legwork, editing the likely ones down, sending the emails and arranging to meet.

- Paid-for sites pre-screen their participants to some degree. As in life offline, there is nothing anyone can do to stop people who don't own yachts claiming they do; or the overweight woman claiming she is a mere size 14; or the rather sad middle-aged man putting up a photo of himself that is a good ten years old. But checks are made behind the scenes so that at least the name on the profile fits the name on the credit card, and the photo is not of some lesser-known movie star or model. Any decent site taking payment from members will also read the profiles, vet the photos (some Russian models turn up surprisingly often in people's profiles) and keep an eye out for those (usually apparently men) who send out hundreds of emails in one day to likely women. (For more on the fraudulent aspects of the internet dating scene, see Chapter 7.)
- At the top end, the more expensive paid-for sites offer something along the lines of the exclusive introduction agencies, though for considerably less financial investment. Clients have to fill out extensive questionnaires and write a 'personal essay' for their profiles, which are then analysed by some complex logarithms, offering matches based on set criteria. If nothing else this process weeds out the half-hearted fling-seekers and will improve your chances of finding a good match, as everyone assumes those signing up and devoting time and energy to this kind of process are looking for a long-term relationship rather than a one-night stand.

There are as many different sites as there are people out there searching . . .

Want fun, sex, no strings attached? Then go into chat rooms, or sign up to the 'free' internet sites, or Google 'adult internet dating'. Free sites for dating rather than casual sex, there's plenty of them around. Are you married and want to meet partners for affairs, love, casual flings? Then you can try any number of sites. One even calls itself the extramarital dating agency for the currently married. A friend recently showed me a link to one of our national railway websites, which carries ads as bold as can be for lonely cheating wives looking for partners. Is that why rail travel is so popular these days?

Looking for a rich older man? There are many sites purporting to provide such potential. Or a lover from a different age range than you? Older women looking for younger male lovers? Or just you're slightly older (and admitting it), looking for a similar age range?

There are single parents sites; special religious sites for Christian or Jewish dating; sites for black people, Arabs, Indians; Muslim dating introduction sites. (The rise of online Asian dating services, introductions, marriage bureaus and singles nights is allowing young Asians to choose their own partner. If you are from a Muslim, Hindu or Sikh background they offer a fast, easy and friendly way to make contact with like-minded single people for friendship, romance or marriage.)

Gay lovers are some of the most active online. Serious academic types may be the least active. There are pan-European dating or more expensive sites, with personality tests and some form of analysis, match-making and questionnaires. You'll find very long lists at the back of this book, so I won't give anyone more advertising space here. As any active online dater knows, it's all just one click on Google away.

Different strokes for different folks

Does the amazing over-supply of possibilities make us all happy, or do some of us just not know how to cope with it all? Have human beings ever been so free, been given so many opportunities to meet, mix, bond, have sex or make cyber contact with each other? It can make the eyes glaze over with exhaustion at the very thought, or create a skip of excitement in the heart. It just depends on what type of person you are. One middle-aged man who claims that he signed up to a reputable online site, and then as quickly took himself off again, said:

> *My anxiety level ran quite deep. It was the whole thing about suddenly being deluged with dozens of profiles: 'she's a 94 per cent match for you; you're an 82.6 per cent match for her'. There is so much pressure to choose, so much fantasy involved each time I look at a picture, read a profile. I found it slightly pornographic and highly addictive. And behind all of that is the question 'Do I know what I really want?'*

A young woman of 25, one of the many professional young singles in London, found it a not too dissimilar experience, though her starting point was very different:

As dating queen of London (albeit unsuccessfully), my reason for trying all and every possible method was the same – desperation!

I tried an online dating website for a few months last year. My basic aim was to get on as many dates as I could. It was fun – all the guys I met (about eight in all) were nice guys, and I never had a truly awful evening. But it's always a bit nerve-racking. I was always more worried I wouldn't recognise my date, rather than worried they'd turn out to be a psychopath.

I think it's a reversal of 'normal' dating – because if you meet someone in a bar you know that you fancy each other – you just need to work out if you have anything in common. With internet dating, you know you have things in common but what you don't know is if you'll find each other attractive, which makes the whole thing a bit more awkward.

I have noticed a strange phenomenon in online dating – there is just too much choice, and men who have joined because they don't want to be single any more suddenly realise they can take out a different girl every night of the week if their email chat is good enough. It means sometimes you'll be arranging a second date with someone, and know that they're simultaneously chatting up three other women. I gave it up in the end because I figured it was more like hard work than dating 'normally'.

Are the online dating sites honest or out to rip you off?

There are crooks and fraudsters around in the business (as there are in most businesses), but surprisingly in the five or six years these sites have been around, because customers are wise to what they might or might not expect, the rip-off merchants have mostly been driven out of business. Genuinely, the largest part of the industry is driven by a true desire to help and to bring people together.

One industry analyst (Gordon Smith), who writes a blog reviewing online dating trends, mobile dating and social networking, says there is now a visible backlash against websites that lie or promise too much:

> *People have wised up – nobody really believes that internet dating is a dead-cert way of finding instant romance. We're seeing more companies doing more to ensure that expectations are set at a realistic level. None of the major dating sites in the UK is ripping off their customers. Most are honest and genuinely wanting to help people find relationships.*

As someone else in the business says, 'No one really believes that the technology alone will find you love or romance. We're there to enable that search or eventual meeting.'

The reputable sites have sunk a lot of investment into building up their databases, and for them word-of-mouth recommendation is the most likely source of new customers. After all, if your best friend has just moved in to live with a fabulous new love and she tells you how they met, you're more likely to join that same site, aren't you?

A director of marketing for a major UK quality newspaper, herself a former relationship counsellor, while admitting that its online dating site brings in a very healthy income, says, 'Who else goes into work and finds flowers or champagne has been sent to them with cards, and emails of thanks that they have finally met the man/woman of their dreams and are blissfully happy? We get a buzz out of it all too!'

Doubts about going online

You might be happy using the internet to order your groceries, but would you feel as easy going online to meet a potential partner? There are still plenty of people who fear the internet and doubt its suitability for dating. Graziella is a strikingly attractive, well-dressed, personable, successful 43-year-old businesswoman living in London. She has two children, aged 6 and 12, and is more or less a full-time single mother, as their father is no longer on the scene. Having moved to London from Poland 20 years ago, she has been very successful in business, but not so much in love. The marriage long since broken up, a couple of years ago she decided to make more effort to meet a new man to be part of her life, even though as she says she is quite happy with her current lifestyle:

> *I have lots of girlfriends who use the internet, but it's so time-consuming, they spend hours online every evening going through endless profiles. I can see how it can become disillusioning. I'd also be worried to meet a total stranger off the internet, not to mention the horror at the thought of plastering my photo on a site where everyone can see it.*
>
> *It's almost like going on eBay, putting yourself up to the highest bidder! Or another image that comes to my mind is it's a bit like those women who put seductive photos of themselves in phone*

booths. It smacks of the sex industry. Oh, it gives me shivers just to think about it. I also think that a certain type of man uses the internet, rather like he would a pub or a bar. He's not really looking for a relationship.

But for every Graziella, I would say there are three who have the totally opposite point of view. And age really is no reflector of how open men or women will be to putting themselves up on a human version of eBay.

The fact that we use the internet not only for shopping, travel and looking up train times, but also for social involvement and social networking, means the dating game is just another side to this overall new phenomenon.

Case studies

Now meet Maddy. She is an interesting, serious-minded, highly intelligent woman of 35, who was prepared to send me the Flickr link to her wedding photos even before we met, and to talk about her incredible fast-paced internet relationship with James. But Maddy is certainly unconventional. When I was arranging to meet her, she said she's hard to miss, as a tall black woman with a cropped bleached Afro haircut.

Maddy is the kind of young professional for whom the internet is an integral part of her everyday life:

The internet is my life. I don't watch TV and most of my free time is spent online. I'm quite used to organising my social life online, I use it to: look for somewhere to live; arrange holidays; pay bills; for college research. So there was nothing really unusual in using it to look for people to date online.

Maddy never felt there was anything negative about making use of the facility. At her age, she says, a lot of friends are coupled up, and besides if you're not the ragingly extrovert type (James, now her husband, is quite shy), then how are you going to meet? It never even crossed her mind that internet dating was intrinsically scary. 'You can meet nutters anywhere!' is her view. In fact she always felt totally in control of the situation:

I considered it was up to me to arrange to meet somewhere safe. They could be lying. But then the same would be true of someone I might meet at the bus stop or in a bar. I was never particularly worried. It really is just a way of meeting people. It's not the site's fault if they're not right for you.

Jenni, whom we met in Chapter 1, and who met her 'compatible partner' Tom online, also says that with busy working lives, seeing your friends can be difficult enough, let along trying to meet a potential new partner:

Being busy at work and often working late into the evenings, I'd begun to see my friends in rotation. So if you can't fit your friends into your free time, when the hell do you meet someone new as a romantic partner? It really is that tough working in a big city. The older you become, the harder it gets. By the time I was approaching 40, the men I was meeting were beginning to be full of baggage

> *– ex-wives behind them, families, guilt. I saw a married man for many months, until I woke up to the fact it was the old story, he wasn't really going to leave his wife.*

These views begin to be heard more and more often. We really do rely on the internet now to open up our lives. Otherwise, we might find ourselves stuck with the small crowd of colleagues at work and the same old social circle of friends, who may or not be able to introduce us to likely potential mates.

How many young(er) people these days will confess that the only way they tend to socialise is going clubbing or out to bars? They know that this doesn't lead to good contacts with people, in terms of someone who might become a partner, or a relationship. How many young people admit quite freely that they're fed up with waking up in bed, after getting off with someone late at night, to find they've had sex with a virtual stranger and don't feel good about it? The answer: almost everyone I spoke to (under the age of 40) brought up such comments.

Returning to Maddy, she describes her 'wired-up' way of socialising. A previous boyfriend introduced her to a community bulletin board, a website used by a group of like-minded people, for whom it's a central 'social network' of vital importance in their lives:

> *That's how I've made lots of my friends. We have a reputation for being quite anarchical, sort of left leaning, alternative. It provides a forum for getting together just to go for a drink, on walks, for dinners, etc.*

I started on internet dating, because I'd been married young and changed career in my mid-30s. Now I was back at university studying for an MSc and I didn't really fit in with the social scene of the other younger grads. I began with the obvious well-known sites like www.datingdirect.com, www.udate.com, www.okcupid.com – the last one lets you chat entirely for free. What's funny is I have a lot of friends who also use it and I kept being matched with them. I'd also be out somewhere in London and have people ask if they'd seen me on that site. Sometimes it's hard to believe London can be so small. Eventually I moved on to www.guardiansoulmates.com as a friend recommended it. You get a very high class of dater, that's for sure.

Other people are even more explicit about the way the internet has filled the gap in our social lives. As one young woman, a 29-year-old press officer for a charity, who moved from Australia to live in London five years ago, said without a flicker of embarrassment, 'Why do we do online dating? I guess because we're sick and tired of shagging the same group of friends!'

Mary Ann, like many Australians, is full of energy, fun-loving, very frank and open about her lifestyle:

I'm part of a big group of friends in North London, we're an arty group who are into music and gigs. And we're all into internet dating. It's part of the way of life we lead. I prefer to meet people this way, rather than getting off with someone in a club, getting drunk. The internet is a kind of safe way of getting to know someone, much safer than meeting them for a drink and going back with a complete stranger. I don't know anyone who's met someone in a bar in recent times. That just seems to have gone out of fashion. I can't even imagine now how other people date, how would they meet people?

You start off in London, when you get here from Australia, maybe meet one person and there's a domino-like effect. I've been out with most of my male friends and we stay friends afterwards. But you have to widen out your circle.

Mary Ann has a slightly different story from others, though, because she began online dating ten years ago, when she was at college in Australia, in the days when the internet was in its infancy and websites were much more for swingers, or sex sites. She started using the internet to meet men even in those riskier times, because again she felt the need to widen her circle from the typical uni friends:

When I came over to London, I started using www.gumtree.com, which a few years ago was for people from Australia, New Zealand and South Africa, but now it's really popular and a bit too overwhelming. Now on the Guardian *Soulmates site, there's a lot of what I'd call 'rock 'n' roll' members. Guys and girls are of a similar mindset, there's a way we write about ourselves too. What I like about it is that, even though sex is obviously there underneath the surface, it's also about making new relationships, finding friends, getting to know new people.*

Is there a particular type best suited to internet dating?

Mary Ann seems to be typical of the type of person who finds meeting people online quite easy. Outgoing, gregarious, she studied journalism at university in Australia and loves meeting people and hearing their stories. Very often it's the extroverts, or the self-confessed 'people junkies', who find it all comes as a natural fit, even though the internet also helps shy people overcome their initial nerves and reserve about going out to meet strangers.

It's hard to be dogmatic about who might feel best suited to online dating. Sometimes a person who has been feeling very low and depressed, after the sudden end of a relationship or love affair, finds that the internet offers a lifeline. Maggie, who is in her late-50s and normally quite gregarious, explains how she was plunged into a terrible depression when her long-term partner suddenly ditched her:

> *The internet saved my life. I felt like the rug had been snatched from under me and I was bitter that he'd taken the best years of my life and then dumped me when I was reaching an age where, I thought, it would be impossible to meet another man. I felt quite revolutionary at the time, as this was about five years ago, and a lot of friends were highly critical about my meeting men from the internet. As though they were all going to be mass murderers! At first I only wrote to men online and I would pour out my sad story. One man wrote back and kept sending me funny stories and jokes, it really worked, and I began to cheer up. Quite soon, I realised how nice it was to have people to write to and sometimes talk to on the phone.*

Now meet Jez, who is just over 50 and has been separated, now divorced, from his wife for several years. He started looking on the internet before his marriage had broken up. What would a man of his age have been able to do even 10–15 years ago, he wonders, with a stale marriage, not sure about divorce because of their teenage children? 'Now, I start speaking to a woman on the internet and if I don't want to muck about sending loads of emails, I just ask if they want to meet, go for a drink. That's the only way to find out if you're going to like them or not.'

Jez started out using the chat rooms through AOL. You just enter into a chat forum that takes your fancy, start emailing people, get talking and can arrange to meet up if both want to do so:

Like a lot of guys might find in their late-40s, with my marriage going downhill, it just offered me an incredibly exciting new life. I went on AOL and found all these chat rooms. They're age specific: 'life begins at 40' or '50-something' or '50+ romance', so you are basically within your own age group. If you strayed into a younger group, you'd be caught out. They're also country-based, and you can choose people who live nearby, on a huge variety of themes. I got chatting and that quickly led to meeting. You come out of the chat room and send an instant message (IM) and have a private conversation. Then you realise it's not so strange or awful, as you're all in the same boat.

I have to admit that the initial thrill of meeting someone illicitly, because we were both still married, was a real turn-on and I became quite hooked on that. You're meeting someone you shouldn't, maybe at a hotel, or motel (some of those chains have built their empires on people like me!). It's amazing how open women will be in a chat room. If you met in normal circumstances, you wouldn't jump so quickly into talking about what underwear she's got on. Then there's cybersex, though I have to say that if it was exciting at first, it soon became boring. This is all how I became hooked on meeting people online. Women are up for the whole game just as much as the men. The chat room phenomenon is really liberating. Online conversations move quickly to sex, it's amazing what women will tell you. But then when we meet, there's a natural shyness at first. I'm always respectful face-to-face.

Mostly I talk or meet women around my own age. I'm not that interested in the younger ones, they've got too many problems. But in the main they're women of a similar age and similar socio-economic background. What I like about ladies 45-plus is that they are so confident, sexually and socially, and have no inhibitions. I'm certainly up for it. I've learnt a lot in recent years.

If you're living on your own, it gives you a thrill to come home at night, and go online. It's as though you've got your own virtual bar. So many people are out there looking to meet others. I'd fill in the time between 9 pm–midnight chatting away to ladies.

As Jez then says, being an extroverted sort of bloke, 'I absolutely adore meeting new people. If we end up having sex that's OK. If I happen to meet someone and want to stay with them, well that's a bonus.'

Do women out there, searching for love or romance on the internet, have an equally robust, cheerful view of the whole process? I somehow doubt they do. My own experience has been far less 'Wow, isn't it all great fun?', as it can be hard work and rather taxing. The answer probably lies in the fact there are all sorts of women, and all sorts of men, and nothing will ever please everyone.

Annie, whom we met recently, says she enjoys the online environment and gets a thrill out of meeting people. She too began using the chat rooms, sending flirts and IM messages. It's been useful for her to learn that being a woman in her mid-50s does not exclude her from male interest. But she too mentions the 'addictive' quality of coming home after work and spending the evening, often till very late, in another world 'online':

> *I would be forever checking my email to see who's online. Like many online daters, it becomes a force of habit, or an addiction, to go online late in the evening, about 11 pm, and then I'd become so hooked on it that I might stay there till 2 am. Some people are in every night and seem to be on for hours. Lots of men will be chatting to 12 other women at the same time. In the end, you have to force yourself to be realistic about the whole situation.*

The addictive quality could become dangerous or bad for you

We'll come soon to more detail about how best to use the online dating sites, for maximum benefit. But one area that I find hard to deal with is where men or women are using the internet solely for 'cyber' conversations and never get to meet. For some, that might happen because they live in isolated rural parts; or they are married and can't find good enough excuses to get out of the house; or they're actually disabled but won't open up and be honest. There might be many genuine reasons, but if there are then it's wise to confess all upfront, rather than keeping another party hanging on, waiting for that date to meet to materialise. Maggie said of her experiences in the early days of online dating:

> *It took me a while to realise it's not all easy and plain sailing. At face value, you think, 'Oh, there's all these quite nice blokes out there. Surely someone right for me will soon turn up.' But I found that quite a few men only wanted to write or talk, because when I suggested meeting up they had all these excuses not to. Someone said there's a lot of married men out there testing the waters, but I can't believe it's true of all of them. Middle-aged men are often rather shy and maybe they just feel more comfortable in their fantasy worlds? Whereas another whole group were obviously just out for sex. It took time to work it all out and begin to get a picture of what might be a possibility. You do get wise to things along the way.*

There is in fact a group of internet 'daters' who prefer what is known as 'cyberlove'. You can read about this in a fascinating book, *Love Online* by Aaron Ben-Ze'ev (see Resources). Here, for example, is a 27-year-old woman having an online affair with a young 18-year-old guy:

> *All my friends think I am crazy and they don't understand why I would spend all my time on a computer talking to this guy, when I could be out on real dates. I don't know either. We have never met or spoken. I don't even know what he looks like. All I know is that I am falling like a fool for someone I may never be able to have.*

Online communication may be detached, but it certainly gets the imagination going and arouses real emotions in the people involved. Another example is that of a married man who is having an online affair. That means he has never met this woman, certainly never kissed her, but their sexual passion is high for each other:

> *I've fallen in love with this woman and I have no idea what she looks like. I think about her all the time. I told her I was falling in love with her and she said the same for me. We both fell hard, fast and deep. I was miserable when I wasn't writing or emailing with her.*

Ben-Ze'ev quotes a psychotherapist writing about this phenomenon:

> *Many of us in the real world have never been with anyone who says or does the sexy, exciting things we crave. Cybersex allows us to retreat into our imaginations and experience some of the wild sexual adventures we don't dare do in real life. Cybersex can be a wonderful experience. If done right it can be very physically*

rewarding as well. You describe your actions instead of doing them. Each person tells the other what you're doing, what you want to do and how you feel.

If that kind of imaginary love, passion and romance is what turns you on, then I'm sure you'll be very happy. It's certainly safer than dealing with real live people, bodies, chemistry, and the potential for pain and rejection. But it's not really what internet dating is meant to be about.

Love at first sight, not at first byte . . .

The email connection is good for that initial contact, but is it best to meet earlier rather than later? This is obviously a very common response to the online dating world. Almost everyone I spoke to in researching this book described the unbelievable shock, most often disappointment, of meeting someone in the flesh whom they imagined to be somehow completely different. One of the main dangers of spending too much time online, emailing, texting, maybe even speaking on the phone, before actually meeting, is that you build up an impression of someone that is fixed firmly in your romantic imagination. You might have even started to fall slightly for the person. In your mind, as a woman, you might be fantasising about the home and babies, or if you are older, the holidays abroad together. As a man, you could be imagining how fantastic she will be in bed, how lovely to look at and how she'll laugh at your jokes. Then you meet for that first drink.

Oh dear. How could a man you found so entertaining on email, whose voice sounded so great on the phone, be such a bore, such a let-down? How could this woman you imagined as a blend of angel and vamp be just plain dull? It happens. There is nothing one can say about the experience, other than be prepared for it, move on and tell yourself in future it's not a good idea to spend a lot of time in this mythical cyberworld. Fix up a meeting and get to know the person in real time, warts and all.

Lesley, the actress, reflects on some of her misgivings:

> *For me, the whole idea of online dating happens upside down. The first thing you see is their photo, and the second is how they express themselves in writing. If the man can't spell or has no sense of grammar, you chuck him out of consideration without giving him a chance. Yet that wouldn't be the first box I would check if I met a man in any other way. It would be a long time before you found out he couldn't write a decent paragraph in the normal world! It's all very skewed. Men will press the delete button for a woman whose looks don't jump off the screen to him. But he's never met her, listened to her, laughed with her.*

Both men and women can be quite ruthless in their checklists of criteria by which they decide whether to follow up an online contact or not. Kathy was one of the fortunate people we met in Chapter 1, who found her partner Mark in the early days of going online (they're now expecting their first child and are about to get married). She describes her own brand of ruthlessness in choosing whom to avoid. Even though she had not initially been attracted to her future husband's online photo, she had strong views about the photos men put up online:

> *In the early days of going online I would use their photos to delete people, rather than for initial attraction. For example, if a man puts up a photo of himself with an ex-girlfriend, or a partner, which was badly cropped, or if he was holding a pint of beer or wearing swimming trunks, they were all off my list. I'd checked that I was looking for a 'serious relationship' and wanted children, so I also only wanted to bother with men who wanted the same. I just wasn't in for timewasters.*

Trust and distrusting what people say online

Can you trust what you read online? Do you want the good or the bad answer? We no doubt all lie a little in our profiles. Then, isn't the very act of writing a subjective process? With another hat on, I teach a journalism class and explain how there is no such thing as purely objective journalism. The very act of writing shifts the way we perceive things, from our choice of what we include, or exclude. In Chapter 7, I will write more about the outright fraud that can take place on the internet. But, for now, we have to assume that the sites set up by decent companies, either owned by a well-known newspaper, or by an introduction agency; or sites that have proved themselves by the test of time (such as the bigger and more widely advertised ones); and certainly those that accept payment for membership, will do their best to read through profiles, check photos that are posted up and at least know that the person's credit card works.

Most people will use the odd little white lie to make them seem more attractive. It is rather like creating your CV, in that you're unlikely to talk yourself down. So be prepared to give or take a few years on age; a few inches on the hips; and, for women at least, what their actual hair colour might be. Any large discrepancy, you'll find out when you meet, at which point you might find the excuse for an early bus home.

Most women I talked to seem to have come across men who lie about their height. Here's Maddy: she is 5 ft 8 in (1.74 m) tall, and he claimed to be 5 ft 10 in (1.77 m):

> *I met him at a bar and got there before him. Then I felt a tap on the shoulder and I swear he was about 5 ft 5 [1.65 m]. Why did he lie about something so obvious? Did he think I wouldn't notice? It left me disappointed for myself and I just thought he was silly. Why would I want to be with someone who thinks that's OK? I stayed for a couple of hours, but I could tell he was expecting it to fail anyway. He was highly educated and a musician, so it was all really weird.*

Or Mary Ann:

> *From the site, I initially had six dates in a few months, not a massive amount and I only slept with one of them. I'm getting pickier and choosier as I get older! The amazing thing is that even though*

I'm only 5 ft 2 in [1.57 m], I still found a guy lying about his height. He said he was 5 ft 3 in [1.6 m], and I swear when we met he was under 5 ft [1.52 m]. It made me feel really strange. But now I've met Sam who is 6 ft 2 in [1.88 m], and some people find that odd. It takes all sorts . . .

A lot of men mention women who give a totally false impression about their weight, or age. Men seem to find it easier to take one look from the bar, realise this is a mistake and make a run for it out by the men's toilets. Most women seem to be able to swallow their pride and at least sit and talk to the odd 'frog' for half an hour or so before admitting that it's perhaps best to move on.

But scams, con-men (and women), fraudsters have always been part of our lives. Bigamists, liars, seducers, cheats – we can't blame the internet for all our woes, although it has enabled such tricksters to be more successful. Here is a woman's story about a weird dating adventure, which she now looks back on and wonders why she let herself get so involved.

• • • • • • • • • •

'I bumped into "the Viscount" in a 40s chatroom.'

I was very vulnerable at the time – my mother had died, I was going through divorce and I'd been made redundant and unable to get another job for over a year. I bumped into 'the Viscount' in a 40s chatroom – just 'sitting on the side'. He read my profile and sent an IM. He was very mysterious and kept dropping hints about his status and notable things in his past. He was a fairly well-known playboy back in the 60s and 70s. After a couple of very long phone conversations we arranged to meet for dinner locally to me. He claimed he'd done a police check on me, although I'd not given him my surname or address – he said he'd found out from my phone number. But he did tend to brag rather a lot, particularly about how ruthless he was in business. At the end of the dinner he produced his credit card and waved it under my nose. He was somewhat upset when I mulled over his name, saying it sounded familiar, when all he wanted me to see was that it said 'Viscount'!

Stupidly, I invited him to my holiday apartment in Spain for a week in the summer, by which time I'd known him just over three months and we'd had a few petty disagreements. The week was a disaster. He never paid for anything and encouraged me to run up huge bills. What a freeloader!

Looking back I can't imagine what attracted me – it certainly wasn't his looks – perhaps it was his attentiveness and flattery at a time when I was in a poor state. After I got back, he sent an email suggesting that I could 'dine out on my tales of my brush with nobility'. I responded that 'you may be a peer of the realm but by no dictionary definition could you be called noble'!

• • • • • • • • • •

Whether you can trust people in terms of safety issues, I'll come to in Chapter 5. Ironically, however, there's another type of person who will come online, who is blatantly open and explicit about him or herself, which in itself can lead to problems.

• • • • • • • • • • •

'I don't know where he finds the energy.'

One of the first men with whom Maggie began a relationship, a few years ago when she began her online adventure, was a special kind of Lothario who, from the very beginning, was completely upfront about his own level of expectations or what he was able to offer the women he let into his life:

Over two or three years, I must have met about 30 men, three of whom I've been intimate with in some way or other. One, Greg, has become a real friend: we do have sex, but he makes it very clear he is not up for any kind of one-to-one relationship. Greg still writes me emails, often several times a week, he loves sending out funny jokes to the sort of 'harem' of women he keeps out there.

I first got in touch with him a few years ago, his photo looked great and he's a real eccentric interesting personality. It was the first time I felt 'wow' with anyone I'd seen on the net. He lives several hundred miles away from me, so we agreed to meet halfway. True to his photo, he just looked gorgeous, and I found him amusing, intelligent and attractive. But from the outset he made it clear that if I wanted to get involved then I would be joining this gang of women he sees on a rotational basis. It sounds amazingly arrogant, but he's obviously got sufficient charm to keep it all going. Personally, I don't know where he finds the energy.

Of course, I really fell in love with him. He started writing emails sometimes four or five a day at first, so I fooled myself into thinking the feelings were mutual. When we had sex, it was remarkable. So then I knew why the other women also agree to his terms. I'd gone and fallen for him in a big way, but he keeps his boundaries. I had entered the inner circle, but if ever I wrote to him about my feelings, he'd withdraw or I'd get a ticking off. He'd had a long and faithful marriage and claims he never wants to be hurt again, as he was when she left him for someone much richer and more successful in life. He's also implied that he never had so much, or such good, sex when he was married. That's very likely true, as it is for lots of married people.

Maggie said she eventually gave him up when she faced the fact her expectations or dreams would never be met. Greg's openness about his lack of interest in a permanent close one-to-one relationship is no different from the married person who maybe enjoys a lover on the side, but makes no wild promises about splitting up his or her marriage. Men and women alike can fall victim of this kind of openness, which at first they find attractive, until they listen to the small voice inside warning them that the situation will never change. The internet cannot be blamed for our meeting men or women who fail to match our hopes, dreams or expectations. We have to look within ourselves as to why we might find such people attractive and don't listen earlier to that inner (often very quiet) voice.

• • • • • • • • • • •

How to deal with knock-backs in the online dating world

While there are young women like Mary Ann, who says she find online dating quite easy as you don't have to get too emotionally involved, other women (and men, young or old) don't find it so easy to detach their emotions. For them, the internet seems to offer countless ways of raising expectations, which are then disappointed, ending maybe again in the pain of rejection. What you need, ideally, is a thick skin. If one of those isn't available, then you just have to brush yourself off and start all over again.

This again is Maggie's view after years of dating, which has produced some relationships, but nothing that has lasted more than a few months:

You've got to be tough and willing to take some knocks if you enter this dating game. Each time you're let down, you wonder why and what had you done wrong, or why are you going for the wrong types? Then you have to brush yourself down, try to perk up the self-confidence and go back out there again. What else can I do? I don't want to spend the rest of my life on my own.

Maybe the internet is hindering rather than helping

Is the internet encouraging promiscuity, ruining our chances of finding a true love or partner? That's a view often cited by men or women who have come across quite difficult problems with the online dating scene. The problems all stem from the very openness and vast amount of possible choices there are available. Many sites let you see who is flirting with, or talking to, other people. So where you might have just had a face-to-face date with someone last night and are holding out a secret hope that the person will want to meet you again, what do you do when you go online and see that he/she is actively talking, chatting (and you don't know what they're saying) with someone else?

There's a whole new 'netiquette' that has: a) not been written, and b) even if it were, no one would hold to its rules. This is the brave new world of ultimate possibilities and ultimate freedom. Along with all other freedoms can come pain, fear, hurt and rejection.

One piece of advice is not to jump to conclusions about the motive for someone else's being online. On many sites, if a stranger makes contact with you, out of politeness you might feel you should check his or her profile and at least say, 'Sorry, thank you for being in touch, but no thanks.' If, during that process, the man or woman you met the previous night sees you are online and acts jealously or possessively, this could come as quite a shock.

There really are no rules of engagement, and the best advice is to be as cool, flexible and laid-back as possible. If you blast off an angry email saying, 'I'm hurt to see you back online, when we've only just met', the most likely response in return will be 'I think we should stop seeing each other, as I find you too controlling.'

Women might brand men as two-timing, no-good, sleaze-bags, etc. Men will brand women as sluts, tarts and a lot worse terms I won't go into now. But all we are really doing is expressing our fear, pain, lack of self-esteem, and desperate need to 'belong' to someone else.

It all comes back to your own expectations and trying to find a match for those with someone else. If a man is very light-hearted about the whole dating scene, the likelihood is that he's happy just having short-lived sexual encounters and is not looking for long-term relationships – whatever he might say in his profile.

Jez, who we met earlier, who seems so perfectly at ease with the online scene, describes how so many women misinterpret things and seem to expect a sexual fling to turn quickly into a relationship:

After my wife and I finally separated, I started paying to join proper online dating sites. I made the move from chat rooms, as a way of making a leap to saying 'I really want to meet someone who I might stay with for some time.' But once you're on to those sites, the women are much more open about the fact they want a relationship. I can't tell you how many times I've been in bed with a woman, who will then start talking about 'a relationship'. I just find it a put-off. I'm wise enough to know that just because I might enjoy her in bed now, or her company, I'd probably go right off her if we ever got to move in together!

But before you take away the wrong impression and think that Jez is at ease with the world and will carry on having sexual flings till he's in his dotage, after several hours of talking about this exciting new world he'd discovered ('I can't tell you how my sex life has gone through the roof since I went online'), he suddenly went quiet and the serious side, so well-buried beneath the 'cheeky chappy' exterior, emerged. He explained how he and his wife both went headlong into internet dating, when it became clear their marriage was stale. They each moved on very quickly. She immediately met a man who made her feel wonderful and they had a relationship for two years, which is now over. Jez had one long-term relationship in the first couple of years:

> *After years of not very exciting marriage, you suddenly find yourself making an effort, buying new clothes or giving a woman flowers. It makes all the difference. Perhaps it was a mistake though, that there was all this freedom out there, and the wife and I didn't give it a chance to start over?*
>
> *One of the downsides of internet dating is that it creates this 'sweet shop' effect. You feel you can overindulge and that can become addictive. I mean I have had so much better sex in recent years than ever before. I was a late bloomer in that I lost my virginity quite late by modern standards. So in that sense I have no regrets. But in some ways, I think I might always have it in the back of my mind that I'll go back to her. That's not really good, is it? Oh well, I'm quite confident I'll meet someone else who'll be the love of my life.*

The 'sweet shop' effect is mentioned by many people, obviously those who have not so far had success in finding a long-term partner on the internet. It's a way of expressing dissatisfaction at the ease with which any of us might think, well, that one wasn't perfect, so I'll start looking again at a few more hundred likely candidates!

> *Some people are online every night and seem to be on for hours. Often a man might be chatting to 12 other women at the same time. That's what I mean about the 'sweet shop' effect. I wonder what will happen in the future? The way attitudes are going, I can imagine men and women might marry to have children, but then just have dates, or serial relationships/flings and not settle or commit to anyone else again.*

Online and offline

Is the internet actually stopping us meeting people in the normal 'offline' or 'organic' way? Have we now become slaves to our computers, manically trying to find out who would be the best person out there for us?

I'm not convinced that, in the general heterosexual world, men or women are going out and socialising less, just because they are looking up potential partners on the internet. But one area does seem to have noticed its impact, and that is the gay scene. The internet is perhaps more widely used by gay men and women for dating, than is true for the heterosexual world. The large gay online sites see more traffic than any others. But then many gay people previously faced problems in how to meet up, especially if they were insecure about their sexuality. This story from Angela, who lives on Long Island and works in Manhattan, gives a fascinating overview of the way the internet dating sites are changing the gay community:

I found some dates that were successful on the www. planetout.com site. Even though there are 3 million people living on Long Island and 8 million in NYC, the gay community can be very small at times when you narrow it down. In this sense the web helped me to get in contact with women I had not met or seen previously. It expanded my search and what I was looking for in a partner.

The internet has also put a lot of gay bars out of business, there used to be many more on Long Island as opposed to just ten years ago. Years ago, many people were forced to go to gay bars to meet others. In this sense there seem to be less meeting places for gay people. The flip side to that is not everyone is into the bar scene, and more often than not someone struggling with their sexuality, depression, etc, shouldn't really be around the bar scene anyway. Other gays who date via the internet and don't take it to that extreme can benefit by not missing out on the dating experience and normalising their lives.

The gay sites also open up areas for swingers to explore. Many people in the gay community really despise swingers, bisexuals and other people experimenting, while others welcome it. I think gay people don't like it because they seem to provide a notion that people can be 'straight' five days a week and be 'gay' at the weekends. It sort of gives the gay community a bad name, or validates that it's a behaviour that can be controlled or learnt.

Another dynamic which is mostly seen in lesbian relationships is while one person in the relationship is sure about their sexuality, the other person may be experimenting (or unable to admit their bisexual orientation), resulting in a terrible ending, not because of compatibility but because one partner can not see themselves living the 'gay lifestyle'.

The internet has played a huge role in the acceptability of this, it's becoming almost more of a rite of passage in a very weird sense. Ultimately, used with responsibility, the internet dating sites can be a great resource to help find a partner or know what's going on in the gay community in your area. It can also help people get the support they need. It can give someone the idea that there are a lot of different kinds of gay people out there and that you don't have to fit into any mould. Just because you're a lesbian doesn't mean you have to be good at carpentry work, camping and auto repair. It also doesn't mean a gay man has to love musicals and make-up. If we see how diverse the gay community can be, it can broaden our perspective and your dating pool.

Before we move on into the world of 'offline' dating, and move into more detail about how to go about setting up your online profile and arranging that first date, maybe it is time to take another quiz and see how you are shaping up in this brave new world of dating.

Quiz

Test your online dating potential

So you think you have what it takes to cause a stir in dating cyberspace? Perhaps your chat-up techniques are second to none but would that be enough? Would you have the right strategies and techniques to hook a hot date online? Take this quick quiz to find out if you've got it all covered.

1. *Everyone seems to be internet dating – even celebrities have tried it. You decide to give it a try. How would you choose which website to go for?*

   a) I'd put my profile on a few different ones and hope for the best.

   b) I'd go for one of the ones that I've seen advertised a lot.

   c) I'd get a recommendation from a friend.

   d) I'd carefully look for the sort of site that would attract like-minded people.

   e) I'd go for the one with the fittest looking members.

2. *You're filling in your profile and it's very tempting to exaggerate or skim over one or two of your attributes. What would you be most likely thing that you'd tell a little white lie about?*

   a) My age.

   b) My marital status.

   c) My children.

d) My height: maybe just add an inch or so.

e) My figure or build: 'curvaceous' sounds so much better than 'could lose a couple of stone'.

f) My occupation.

g) Alcohol intake: I think 30 units a week could come under the label of 'occasional drinker'.

3. *When you're filling in the profile it's all much more time-consuming than you'd realised. How would you find the time to finish it all?*

a) I'd give up and do it another time if it took more than an hour.

b) I'd just finish it off quickly without thinking about it too much.

c) I'd miss out some of the detailed questions – I suppose I could always fill them in later.

d) I'd probably leave out all the optional sections.

e) I'd finish it properly and think about how I want to come across even if I had to stay up late to do it.

4. *Which of the following would you be most likely to put in your profile (try to choose one even if you don't think it would be any of them)?*

a) I work hard and I play hard.

b) I like nights out and romantic nights in.

c) I like going to the cinema and watching DVDs.

d) I have a good sense of humour.

e) I love watching trashy TV/sitcoms/reality TV.

5. *You're choosing a photo to put on your profile. Which one would you go for?*

   a) There's a great one of me and my ex on holiday. It's not showing too much of his/her face so I'd use that if it was the best one I had.

   b) I don't really have many digital photos of myself so I'd just take one myself with my mobile phone.

   c) A picture of me at a wedding. At least I've got a nice outfit on.

   d) A stylish black and white photo.

   e) Something sexy which shows off my body.

   f) If I didn't have a decent head and shoulders shot, I'd get a friend to take a photo of me.

   g) I'd be tempted to put on a photo from a few years ago – well, I probably don't look all that different.

   h) Something blurred or taken from a distance.

6. *You've posted your profile. What's your strategy next?*

   a) Wait for people to approach me. I wouldn't want to appear desperate.

   b) I'd go through loads of profiles and mark out loads as my favourites and hope they get the hint.

   c) I'd choose one that I liked the best and send the person a message.

   d) I'd probably send out messages to a couple of people.

   e) Send out identical (but well thought-out) messages to as many people as took my fancy.

7. *Supposing you decide to contact someone. What would you put in your initial message?*

   a) Give a general introduction, explain a bit about myself and ask them a few questions and hope they get in contact.

   b) Something obviously sexual and flirtatious.

   c) Just a simple, maybe cheeky, question about something in their profile.

   d) A few paragraphs about myself, my relationship history and what I'm looking for in a mate.

8. *So the person you liked the sound of has been replying to your messages. What do you think would happen next?*

   a) After exchanging a few messages we would probably start emailing then maybe exchange mobile numbers. I'd try and chat to him/her on the phone before too long.

   b) I'd want to have a flurry of emailing so we felt like we were really getting to know each other before meeting up – that feeling of being able to ask each other anything and everything.

   c) After a couple of messages I'd like to suggest meeting up on a date.

   d) I'd like to know the main reasons why his/her last relationship broke up before we exchanged phone numbers.

9. *When it comes to arranging the date, what could you see yourself saying?*

a) I don't mind. What do you want to do?

b) Do you want to meet for a coffee or something – that way we don't have to make a big night of it if we don't like each other?

c) I know this great little Italian near me.

d) Do you like going to the cinema?

e) I know a great dim sum place we can go for lunch.

10. *Would you see yourself texting each other before the date?*

a) Yes, I think it's great to get a bit of cheeky banter going beforehand.

b) Yes – probably just to confirm the arrangements.

c) Yes – I think it could be good to get the flirtation going on early and tell him/her all about why I'm so good in bed and what underwear I'm wearing.

d) Texting?! I'd probably be sending a semi-clad picture of myself.

e) Not really – I'd rather wait to see if we fancy each other first.

f) Yes – constant texting shows we're both really keen.

Your answers

1.	a) 1	b) 2	c) 3	d) 4	e) 0			
2.	a) 1	b) 0	c) 0	d) 2	e) 3	f) 1	g) 4	
3.	a) 1	b) 2	c) 1	d) 0	e) 4			
4.	a) 0	b) 1	c) 1	d) 2	e) 4			
5.	a) 0	b) 1	c) 2	d) 1	e) 2	f) 4	g) 0	h) 0
6.	a) 0	b) 1	c) 3	d) 4	e) 1			

7. a) 2 b) 1 c) 4 d) 0
8. a) 4 b) 2 c) 1 d) 0
9. a) 2 b) 0 c) 4 d) 1 e) 4
10. a) 4 b) 3 c) 0 d) 0 e) 2 f) 2

Scoring

Hot stuff (32–40)

Either you're a pro and you've done this before or you're a natural. There's not much that you need to be taught about internet dating, so what's stopping you? You're bound to meet people to go on dates with in no time.

Definite room for improvement (14–31)

Good, but you could do better. You have some definite strengths but you need to make the most of yourself right from the start. You probably just want to meet the right person for you rather than going on hundreds of dates, so why not do things properly if you're thinking of spending money on it?

You need to go back to the basics (0–13)

OK. You've got a lot to learn. Perhaps you're really not up for a relationship at all? Or maybe you're not interested in possibly meeting the love of your life?

But for everyone else, there's an etiquette to internet dating and if you're going to make the effort, you may as well do it properly and learn how to not waste your time.

These are my top tips for internet dating:

- Choose one site, and choose carefully. Think about the sort of person you want to meet.
- Write your profile carefully, and allow it to express something of your personality.
- Avoid clichés (work hard, play hard) and empty phrases such as 'I like reading.' It's much better to say 'I'm passionate about literature.'
- You need to sound upbeat, passionate (not in a sexual way – always keep sex out of your profile), positive and friendly. Try describing your ideal day or your dream holiday, or your perfect night out.
- And a word about the truth. Don't lie. Especially never lie about your age, occupation, marital status or children. Any potential boyfriend/girlfriend would be entitled to tell you to get lost if they found out.
- A great photo is much more important than you think. Make the most of yourself, then get someone to take a clear digital photo of you (head and shoulders). You can't afford to get this wrong.
- Don't wait to be contacted. Make the first move, but take your time and be selective. Don't send loads of messages at the same time – you could be inundated and not have time to do it properly.
- Be brief in your initial message. Always ask a question, and be specific to the person's profile. Preferably make them smile, but at least spark an interest.

- At the next step you should just exchange a few brief messages before slightly longer ones. You need to engage the person and make them interested. There's no need to give away too much too quickly and send really lengthy emails. Then move to emails and mobiles for texting or phone calls (only if you feel it's safe). Don't wait too long to suggest a date.

Chapter 4

Other Ways of Dating: Beyond the Internet (or Offline)

Despite the hype, believe it or not, going online to internet dating sites is not the only way to find a date. There may be some 6 million singles (well, we hope they are all single) who have signed up to the hundreds of online sites, but the vast majority will also be pursuing other methods of dating, meeting potential partners, or just having a social life outside their own small circle of friends.

As Leila, a woman in her early-40s whom I came across at a singles cookery evening, said, 'You never know when you'll bump into the right man, so you really do have to carry on with life and get as much out of it as possible. I go out whenever I can, to singles events and through a singles network. There's no point in waiting at home for something to happen!'

Leila has joined a group for young, or middling-to-young, professionals who meet to go to the theatre, dances, country walks and even holidays. She's made some good friends that way, and doesn't mind if at times it's just two or three of the women who might get together to go out dancing. The aim is not to be a 'desperate dater', but to be sociable, relaxed, flexible and the kind of person who is open to new adventures.

Another woman who also tries out events and goes to a lot of singles nights that are held in pubs in central London (and all other major cities nationwide), reckons the reason such face-to-face events are more successful for her is that she doesn't come across well on internet dating sites, indeed, because of her appearance. I was rather shocked that Beverley said that, as she's a very attractive smart black woman with a career in the health profession. This is how she explains her internet problem:

> *I'm 42 and I know I don't look my age. I've never been married and don't have kids. My profile doesn't work well on an internet site. If I give my right age, that puts off younger men who I might find more fun. Men tend to assume there must be something wrong with me, for not conforming to type! They always ask why I've never been married. I prefer to go to singles events and meet people socially. I find socialising easy and enjoy talking to people. I like the kind of evenings where a group of singles meet in a bar, just chatting and getting to know people. It's more relaxed, a better way of meeting people.*

As I mentioned in Chapter 2, if you are shy and retiring, sometimes forcing yourself out to a singles event or social evening can be a good way of trying to overcome the shyness. After all, everyone there will also be a self-confessed singleton, looking either for company or perhaps to meet someone special, so there really is no need for embarrassment.

The old, tried and tested ways to meet people have always been along the lines of: you go in a group, or just with a friend, to a pub, bar or to a party. You hope that friends in couples will invite you over for Saturday evening dinner or Sunday lunch, when there will be some other singles present. Weddings have traditionally been a happy hunting ground for meeting potential partners, as they bring together two wide circles of contacts and friends, often from all over the world. The only problem with weddings is everyone tends to get rather drunk!

Friends are the best bet for helping you meet someone, so do be honest with as wide a circle of people as you possibly can reach, and let them know you are now actively looking, that your days of TV watching are over. Ask them outright if they know of anyone to maybe fix you up with. Friends who are in couples might know a young guy who has recently split up with his girlfriend. But as he might be the pal of your girlfriend's fiancé, there's no way you would ever have known about him. Your cousin might know someone through her church group or sports club. The boundaries really are limitless. Just as I described in Chapter 1, the randomness of meeting a new partner, or soul mate, is so bizarre and weird, that however you get to meet really makes no difference.

I used to know a charming male colleague, who in his mid-30s seemed to be dallying with several women, unable to settle down. Then one day travelling on the London Tube he spotted an amazingly striking and attractive tall woman. After eye-balling her for the 15–20 minutes they sat opposite each other, when he saw her getting up to leave, he slipped her a piece of paper with his mobile number. She called. The rest, as they say is history. They've been together ever since, helping and supporting each other through career changes, flat hunting, all the time so evidently very much in love.

We all tend to lead such busy lives in major cities, seldom looking each other in the eye as we hurry by. Here Sally, a young journalism student from New York, writes about a chance encounter that happened to her a few years ago.

'You never know what will happen if you disturb the natural flow of this busy New York way of life. What would happen if you just stopped in front of someone who's hurrying somewhere? I once had a stranger block my way and I thank God he did.

My friends and I were out in Harlem one night, living care-free, the way we usually did on weekends, looking for a lounge with good music and good drinks to spend the rest of the night in. As we approached Lenox Avenue, I encountered a young man: very tall and extremely handsome. He smiled at me. I blushed, smiled back and shyly glanced downward. He approached me and we struck up a conversation. It felt right talking to this man, who I'd never met before. Yet still part of me felt awkward. What would my mother think if she saw me hav-ing a conversation with a stranger? But there was just something about him – I couldn't end our conversation, we clicked. We exchanged phone numbers and said our goodbyes. Those 15 minutes spent have now stretched to a few years of us being together. We fell in love with each other. We've made each other laugh and cry. We've helped each other through conflicts, and we've conflicted. He and I turned into we.'

Try the odd blind date. Follow up all sorts of leads. Treat this venture as you would trying to find a new job. Endeavour to meet or talk to someone new or different at least once a week. Just dragging yourself out to different arenas can be the best way to meet people. Go on singles holidays, or even more adventurously, go on holiday on your own and make sure you get talking to new people. Take up a new sport. Or go to work voluntarily in the Third World for a few months. Break the mould. Get out of the box. Take yourself out of your comfort zone.

Whether to do the chat, or let yourself be chatted up

There is absolutely nothing wrong with daring to talk to a complete stranger, woman or man, so long as you don't expect an instant successful response. When young people have said so often, during my interviews, that they hate the business of being chatted up in a pub or bar by some drunken young man (or vice versa), the important word there was the 'drunken' part. No woman of any age will find it flattering when a man is leering over her, staggering with glass in hand, maybe making coarse comments or staring too obviously at certain parts of her body. If the two of them do end up going back to one of their flats for a night of something masquerading as passion, then the odds are on that one or the other will wake up in horror, grab their clothes and make a run for it. They certainly won't be exchanging phone numbers!

But there is an art and a skill to making a brave attempt at striking up a conversation with a stranger, who you think might be an interesting person and who you hope might be interested in you. In my own life, I met the new love of my life in the most unexpected circumstances. Alone and feeling very miserable at my single state, I'd gone to spend a week by an Italian coast, in rather too much solitary confinement. With just a few days to spend, I didn't feel like going with a girlfriend or trying to persuade other family members to come with me this time. Maybe subconsciously, I knew it was time to face up to my solitary status and think it all through. The only problem was I had way too many hours for all that thinking. I'd left my mobile phone charger back in the United Kingdom and there was no easy access to email. I was beginning to lose touch with the outside world. Panic! Rather like an addict who hits rock bottom, I was about to plateau on solitude.

That morning, unable to face the hot sun on the beach until later in the afternoon, I told myself I had to be out and about, not hiding away in my little holiday flat. So I 'braved it' to the terraced café in the village square. That might sound stupid, but whereas it's easy to go to a Starbucks et al in any major city worldwide on your own, to go into a small village café, where the local old men hang out and stare mercilessly at a stranger in their midst, I found excruciating. I'm sure their staring was merely out of fascination or boredom, but it was as though they compounded my solitary status by silently saying, 'Why is that woman on her own?'

Imagine my surprise when a young man with long curly hair sitting at the next table started to try to draw me into conversation. I was obviously not Italian, and my lack of the language confirmed that. When I was ordering my coffee (an Americano), he decided I must be American? No. Well, German? Good guess. No. I said, in my best Peggy Ashcroft voice, 'Sono Inglese' – I knew that much Italian at least. But he persevered with his efforts at making conversation. I explained I was going to the nearby town in my car to try to find an internet café. He offered to come with me and be my guide. My natural instinct was to think, 'This guy is taking the piss. What does he think he's about? He's way younger than me.' If I'd been there with a girlfriend or anyone else, I'd have shouldered him away, perhaps after a lot of flirting and giggling.

But something stopped me being so cold and thoughtless. I gave in and accepted his offer of taking me to the next town. In broken Italian, with a smattering of German (from far-off GCSEs), we began to communicate. I won't go into detail, but he's the best thing to have come into my life for many years.

I wouldn't recommend going on holiday on your own as a sure-fire way to meet someone. I could just as easily have continued lonesome and bored. But in a way I did encourage fate to step in and make a stand. As one of my single women friends commented when I came home and replayed the story, 'That's why we have to be brave and go places on our own sometimes. If you're always with a friend or other companion, you have too many excuses not to get to know someone. It's too easy to fall back into normal patterns of behaviour and lifestyle.'

Why someone might be far more open to 'chat up' offline

I came across an interesting viewpoint from a mid-40s man who was writing on a blog site about the difference between internet dating and the offline version, which actually sums up the reasons that it can be good to force yourself out into the open. It means you have to make that special effort to talk to a stranger. It takes you away from the assumed air of self-confidence, that you can so easily put over when writing on the internet or by email, to the reality of your shyness or emotional attitude. And, despite our avowed aversion to being chatted up, most women (and maybe some men) are really quite flattered when someone makes such a Herculean effort. Why? Because we all know how hard it can be.

This is from an American blog: 'Why do really great women who rule you OUT online, rule you IN offline?'

From women the responses went along these lines:

- Men have no shame online. Although most men might be afraid to approach you in person, they don't have an issue approaching you on dating and social networking sites.
- We don't trust the men we meet online.
- Men email us for only one thing (they want sex) . . . at least we can pretend in the real world, when they ask us out, they want us for more than that!
- Asking women out offline is a manly thing to do. And most women appreciate manly things. Asking a woman out in broad daylight takes confidence . . . I like confidence.

And this fascinating response from a man:

> *I dated online for about four years and got really good at it. But it was still frustrating and it was a crap shoot no matter what. Then I quit online dating to learn to approach women in the real world. This has changed my life immensely. I have become much better, more confident, comfortable and more myself around women. When I walk up to a girl in the park or on the subway train and start talking to her, there's instant attraction, because she knows how hard it is for guys to do this. I was scared as hell at first. But I learned how to do it by going out constantly.*

I think those few words of his tell all about the real nitty-gritty of what dating is about. Facing up to your own inner fears. Being brave even when you may not feel it. Really working out what kind of woman, or man, appeals to you and finding the inner confidence to go up to that person to let them know you're attracted and why. Then moving ahead slowly, so you take time to get to know them. You're not just out to get them into bed for the night and then goodbye. You want to know them as a whole person and just maybe spend some years, or even – if lucky – the rest of your lives, together.

Options and expectations

So am I saying that if we meet someone in more traditional ways, the path to true love is likely to run more smoothly? Sorry if you're getting that impression. The sad truth is that the same pitfalls abound for offline dating as for online. And why is that?

Because exactly the same overload of hope and expectations can come into play, which far exceed the reality of the likely situation.

You meet someone at a party. He/she seems to be attracted, even entranced by you. You exchange phone numbers and agree to see each other again. Your heart flutters, you can almost feel the sand under your feet on that first holiday to an exotic resort. Maybe the person does phone, two or three weeks later. You go out again. This time you spend the night together. Then he/she doesn't phone again. Sounds familiar?

• • • • • • • • • • •

'In New York, there are so many beautiful girls.'

This story of Annabel, a gorgeous-looking, lively, outgoing 29-year-old from London who is now working most of the year in New York, will ring rather a lot of bells for many women (and possibly men too, who can find themselves in similar ungratifying situations):

Living and working between New York and London, the two greatest dating capitals of the world, I know tons of people who do internet dating, I've just never got round to it, nor do I really want to. It's not that I'd be afraid or anything like that. It gives you plenty of chance to clear up their credentials, like age and income before you meet. I just can't see myself having the time that's needed to invest in it. I've never been on a blind date either.

Generally I meet people through friends or even randomly on the street. I've had just one real relationship since I've been in New York and that's in about six years. I met him by chance on my first day here. He's Norwegian, so that made him different. But it doesn't usually happen like that.

Dating in New York is certainly interesting, but unpredictably predictable. In many ways, it would appear to be easier to meet people here than in London, because everyone goes out more. They all go to bars, restaurants and stay out late. You're with a crowd of people. But it's definitely more superficial than in the UK. I'd say you don't really get to know the men well at all.

Worse, in New York, there are so many beautiful girls. They reckon in Manhattan there are five women to any one man. So the guys have a lot of choice. The men don't commit and can treat women as they like. They don't have to make much effort, as there are so many really interesting, intelligent, beautiful and dynamic young women around. It's all work, gym, tennis, skiing. A girl can be fitted in between 10 pm and midnight and the guy will feel no responsibility towards her or her feelings.

In Annabel's case, I'm not sure why she puts up with it. I did ask her why she hadn't started looking to date men from elsewhere, other than New York, if the odds were so stacked against making a relationship there? I get the feeling that in a few years time, when she is seriously starting to think about making a family with someone, she will cast her net wider. I even hazarded the suggestion she look in Wyoming or New Jersey – anywhere that she could find men who were looking to meet a 'real' woman rather than some arm-candy for a one-night stand.

• • • • • • • • • • •

So let's get things straight. Whether you also try internet dating, or not, if you make great efforts to pursue some of the more inventive ways of dating that are being dreamed up, even as I write this, there are still no hard-and-fast guarantees. But at least by getting out more, doing different things, you will be enjoying life along the way, gaining some valuable experience, meeting new people and hopefully building up the self-confidence that will make things snowball so one day you will meet that 'right' person.

I feel that the world of 'offline' dating breaks down into age-related sections, far more so than 'online' dating. The internet is, in the first place, set up to divide people into age categories, and then the two people organising a date will veer towards the kind of situation or event that suits them best. In the offline world, there are singles events that are only ever going to appeal to the young, and similarly the not-so-young and the just-getting-on-a-bit types. So I'm going to look at the various types of dating scenarios for these three groups. Please don't read this to mean I'm excluding anyone from getting involved. If you're game, then try anything once.

You're 20s to mid-30s

The most commonly experienced dating situation in this age group is the now almost ubiquitous speed dating. Several speed-dating organisations have been set up all over the nation and they mostly advertise on the internet (see the Resources section for some of their websites). They will limit different evening events to different age groups, usually with a final cut off for those in the mid-40s. The business has become hugely popular, with one organisation operating 30 events a week, in different locations, with thousands of active members. It's another version of that random selection, offering you another roll of the dice.

Speed dating seems to suit young professionals best. Maybe it reflects university life a little, when most socialising was done in bars, or at music concerts, where the level of noise was extremely high. It may sound callous at first, that you will get to meet anything from around 15–30 random strangers, with whom you can talk for all of three minutes, and expect to come away with a distinct impression of those you might want to see again, but once more, this is a reflection of real life. Where we might not all be the type to fall in love at first sight, it's obvious that it can happen. And in a reflection of that other interview situation we've all been through, for a new job, we're probably used to the concept that an interview panel might take all of 30 seconds to sum up a new candidate, and will have more or less made up their minds about you before the questions even begin.

The main trick about speed dating is to try to find groups that will best suit your own lifestyle and attitudes. You can do that by visiting their websites or phoning up the organisers and talking to them about the kind of people who go along. Another plus point for speed dating is that it is relatively cheap, as you're not involved in paying for dinner. You go to a well-known restaurant or bar and a few introductory drinks are included in the price. By mid-evening, you can either slope off home or gang up with some others to go for a meal. Your feelings might come away relatively unscathed so long as you don't take the reactions of your fellow daters to heart. Some more sensitive souls have described it as 'pure hell', in that you can be rejected by 20 or more people all in the same evening! Cards are marked as to your rating, and you do the same for the people you've met. If there's a match in interest, then you can arrange to meet up with that person again. You might even be given the phone number or email of someone you met there, by the organisers, to make another stab at getting to know them afterwards.

The Chinese, by the way, may have hit the nail on the head – in terms of getting together the largest group of people for speed dating. Five thousand men and women met in a Shanghai park for a huge speed-dating event. They were all aged 20–45 with a level of further education. Each participant had a rose, to hand over to someone they found attractive. If they were too shy to do the handing of the rose themselves, they could ask Cupids to deliver the flower or a message. I suppose it would be a rather like going to Glastonbury and knowing that everyone else there was single – and looking for a partner! To some that could indeed be a living purgatory.

Here are a few comments from some typical mid-20s professionals who have tried speed dating in recent months.

• • • • • • • • • • •

'I'd definitely recommend speed dating.'

Alistair, 27

I went speed dating a few months ago, after a few friends said they'd been. I asked around some others to see if they'd come along, but they bottled it and made feeble excuses about being busy, washing their hair or not being over their exes yet. So I decided I'd go on my own. I was a little nervous but kind of excited as I enjoy doing random things like this.

I'd definitely recommend speed dating and would go again. The night itself was great fun, as long as you don't take it too seriously and don't expect too much. If you are the type who is afraid to approach men or women in bars (which does take a lot of guts), then it's ideal as everyone is open and friendly and the situation is very relaxed. However, in terms of finding a 'perfect match', well, that's just as much down to luck as it is in real life!

Alistair has worked out a few theories from his experience, which are telling in relation to what I have been talking about previously:

- *Women hunt in packs. All of them were with friends, none would dare go on their own. Men, on the other hand, were all on their own. I thought I'd be the only one, but all the other guys were alone too.*
- *The women were all normal, pleasant and generally fun. Some of the guys, however, were a little odd, and without wishing to sound harsh, you could see why they had taken up speed dating.*
- *The women were generally younger than the men, on average about 23–24. The men were 25–30.*

I found the individual dates went by quickly. There was the occasional break in between, but there were about 14 dates. It did take some effort to think of original things to say, especially when the women always ask where you are from and what you do.

With the formalities over and the dates all done, what I thought would be the best bit was a little disappointing. I expected the mingling over a few drinks afterwards would be far more interesting and fun. But most of the women left straight away and few stayed beyond half an hour. I think that was because it was a week-night, but still annoying! That left a group of slightly drunk lads and we all went out to another bar for a few drinks. Not what I'd imagined would happen before the night began, but I wasn't going to say no to a few more beers.

Buoyed on by the theme of the night, some guys decided they were going on the pull. It was a great example of how not to impress women. They were drunken, lairy and most girls walked away or ignored them. I stayed well clear of that bunch, and as the crowd died down, made my way home.

When it came to matches, over 50 per cent of the women had ticked me as a friend or dating match. To be honest, I was only interested in one of those, and we met up afterwards for a date. Trouble was, the fact we had met by speed dating was our biggest problem. We had so little in common it was awkward. This girl didn't drink alcohol, tea, coffee or fruit juice. She drank water or Coke, which made finding a venue for our first drink very tough. We had a nice enough afternoon, but both knew we weren't interested in each other.

Rachel, 34

A friend and I decided to give speed dating a go quite recently. It had been a while since I'd been dating (recovering from the end of a relationship), and I wanted to 'practise talking to boys'.

We decided to approach the evening just as a fun night out, without building up any expectations. We met about 21 men, for three minutes each, and I did indeed get to 'practise talking to boys'. For most three-minute periods we managed to chat away without having to resort to my 'killer question' (for me, 'What do you like to read?'). I actually bumped into someone I knew there, which was slightly embarrassing, but when we had to do our three minutes we just compared how the evening was going for each other.

The main problem on the night was that out of 21 men I only fancied two of them. Then I got to talk to one of them more informally after the speed-dating part of the evening had ended and decided he wasn't on my wavelength at all. Still, he seemed to like me, which was a boost.

The next day was a totally different question. The scoring process is your chance to be turned down by up to 21 men! In fact, I was turned down by 17 men, and half of those 17 didn't bother to score anyone, so there's some consolation there, but still it's not a nice process at all. I did get one match however, and we met up for a date. Although we didn't click, that date left me much more positive about dating in the future.

My decision – one-on-one dating is the way forward for me (and the only way I know to do this is internet dating). You genuinely get to find out about someone, and make your decision on whether to see them again not just on a first three-minute impression. If you're just after a fun night out, and can handle the potential rejections the next day, speed dating could be for you.

Just so we have plenty of male voices offering their view (women, as usual, talk far more easily about anything to do with dating, love, romance and sex), let's hear it from Richard, 27, who gives a witty and erudite overview on the process as experienced by a young academic in Edinburgh:

Everyone was making fun of my friend James for going speed dating. For moral and social support I said I'd go along; plus I'd never done anything remotely like speed dating before and was tired of reading about the world rather than living it.

I met James along with his friend Sarah. We were shown to our seats in a rather gloomy bar underground in the darkest depths of Edinburgh. A card was passed around upon which we were to commit our most intimate feelings gleaned over a four-minute meeting with each participant of the opposite sex. I decided that actually writing down anything in front of someone you'd just been introduced to was beyond rude, so devised a code for each of the important bits: this worked badly.

Early drinks with James aside, the evening was an exhausting and barely memorable experience: the card and full use of it was essential. Most of the women were either doctors or worked for Royal Bank of Scotland. The guys, apart from James and me, were for the most part on a stag night. I made no sense of this but it gave a useful conversation piece beyond 'What's your favourite root vegetable?' A potato, incidentally, is a tuber.

By the end of the evening I had been forbidden from discussing the environment by an environmentalist, attempted to discuss COBOL syntax with a programmer (and thankfully failed), and agreed with by far the nicest person I met that, although speed dating is a worrying sign of desperation in all but the busiest people, it is at least more human than finding folk over the internet. In retrospect this was the only point we agreed on, as she failed to tick me.

Speed dating appeared entirely unrelated to real life, rejection coming with none of the conventional pain. The awkwardness was mutual, and in some perverse way enjoyable, as you knew it couldn't possibly be your doing. I met some nice people and was pleased to discover that outside academia people are pleasant and attractive. I'd go again, but not on my own (or on a stag night), as one would run the risk of feeling desperate.

• • • • • • • • • • •

Back with modern methods that try to bring people together, the younger age group are also most likely to enjoy, or try out, a variety of novelty tricks. You have to face the fact, that whatever the name of the game, the organisers are merely helping you out by arranging the icebreaker situations. This wave of new dating games has come to the United Kingdom from the US, where the post-*Sex and the City* women (or those described by Annabel) have determined that the best way to meet men is to get out there, hunting.

There are **lock and key** parties, which sound smuttier than they are (the name is reminiscent to me of those car key events where swinging couples would put their keys in a bowl and go home with a stranger!). Lock and key parties often take place in top restaurants, can attract up to 200 participants, and have the resonance of a rather fashionable party. Every woman has a lock dangling around her neck. The men move around the room with keys that they can try in the locks until they find one that opens. The compatible pair may then decide to spend the rest of the evening together, or they can smile inanely and the woman can request a new lock. The main aim is to bring people together in a non-threatening way. While you consume a few drinks, you just might find someone whose number you wish to take away, or even fix to go for dinner later that evening.

You might like to try **dinner in the dark**, a most unusual way to go about eating, let alone meeting anyone, as you literally eat in a darkened room, finding the food with your fingers and no doubt knocking over the wine glass too. By depriving diners of one of their senses, organisers say you worry less about your looks or what you're wearing (or indeed, what they are wearing). There are a few restaurants around offering this 'pleasure'. You meet in a lit bar for a drink, then a small group of six or eight men and women are taken into the darkness by a waiter who is helped by night vision goggles. By the dessert course, they bring candles to the table and you get your first glimpse of your fellow guests. Not for the claustrophobic or faint-hearted.

Men and women seem to enjoy wine-tasting with equal gusto, so a **wine-tasting party** can be a good option as a way to spend an evening with other singles. The cost is relatively low, as it does not include dinner. The venues are usually quite upmarket, and your ticket will cover tasting of eight wines (champagne will cost extra) and some sandwiches. For every wine that is tasted, experts will give different descriptions and your singles team will have to decide which is correct. Throughout the evening, teams break up and move around, so that everyone gets to mingle with all available people. Contact cards are around so that you can exchange phone numbers or emails.

Singles holidays and **adventure weekends** can be very popular outings. You don't have to sign up for a whole holiday week with strangers, but might go for a weekend break – **speedbreaking** – with a mystery group of single people. Or adventure weekends can be a lot of fun, based on the 'reality TV' idea, whereby a group of 20 men and women are stranded in the remote countryside and left to battle out the elements, and various sporting activities, together.

If you're not the type to enjoy the rowdiness of speed dating, where the level of both drinking and talking can be quite extreme, then maybe you'd prefer to try a **quiet party**. These dating events are meant to attract the more literary and perhaps old-fashioned of us, as you are handed a pen and notepad, whereby you make contact with people who catch your eye in writing. Rather like the Victorian method of courtship, by coded love letters, this could be a romantic way to approach the singles scene.

Dance dating is very popular among those who just love to boogie, and there are also the singles social groups that crop up in most cities, who organise singles parties in large clubs, bars or restaurants (see the Resources section for a list of the most well-known websites).

Networking in one's own professional sector has long been a method of meeting other people, either for career-motivated reasons or also to meet new friends and just possibly potential partners. Many young people are organising their own **intra-professional networking groups** that will meet in a bar, or organise groups to go to the theatre, or sporting events. These would seem to be ideal for men or women who find that the drink and noise of some dating methods exclude them on grounds of heightened sensibilities.

Graduates also get together either through **alumni associations** of their own Alma Mater – and a lot of those events lead to the pairing-off of new partners, marriages or even divorces. Some enterprising young professionals have also brought together a wide variety of **single graduates** for fun evenings, music, dancing and parties. If you don't know of one in your area, then set one up yourself: that way you will also get to meet a whole lot of new people!

If travel is important to you, then you might want to advertise in the personal columns or on the internet for **travel companions** (best to make it into a group) who will all go away together. Or, perhaps if you're feeling jaded at work and in your love life, maybe it's time to take a year out, a belated gap year, and go off to work with **voluntary organisations** overseas. You just might meet your partner out there too.

You're mid-30s to late-40s

Forgive me if I'm jumping to conclusions here, but I am working on the assumption that you might have become tired by now of the casual late-20s style of dating. You might well have already been married, lived with someone in a close relationship for several years, or are a single parent, either with the children more or less full time or in the shared parenting situation, before finding yourself back on the dating scene again. In previous chapters, we've come across plenty of people in the same boat who have had to force themselves back out there 'on the market' again. So you are not alone – even if it feels that way to you.

There are plenty of valid reasons for you to go to speed-dating events, as most of the organisers offer specific groups for your age range, and indeed some daringly take the age limit up to 55. (I still wonder why the cut-off age has to be so brutal? Are they afraid of a roomful of 'oldies' putting off the younger ones?)

One speed-dating outfit in fact grew out of a long-standing corporate networking operation called 'keycontacts'. Members showed that they were looking to have a similar form of speed dating, but this time to meet the needs of many owners of small businesses, or freelancers, who were frankly hoping to meet potential suitable partners, less for the boardroom than the bedroom. The clientele's age ranges from 35 to 55 (and no doubt some older ones sneak under the wire too). Other speed-dating outfits also hold special evenings for the 40-plus age group. Professional networks, alumni associations, tracing old school-friends, hobby-related activities, or just singles social evenings might suit you best.

Often by the time men or women have reached their early-to-middle years they begin to feel the pace of time marching on – and that's not only women looking at declining childbearing years either – and they begin to focus more intently on the need to find a good partner in life, without the time-wasting that can go on in the casual social arena. If you are well-established in your career, time becomes the single most difficult factor. So if you are cash-rich and time-poor, then it's a good idea to look at other methods of dating that might involve some financial investment but will make best use of your beleaguered time allowance.

There are all sorts of ways that you could make just this investment. One is to sign up and join a social group that will arrange **dinner dates** or **social events** with like-minded, similarly professional people and others on some kind of equal financial footing. There are a few such organisations (again you will find their websites listed in the Resources section) with healthy subscription lists of members in the several thousands. If waiting to meet a stranger under the clock at a station is no longer for you, then these types of events, which can be pricey (from say £75–100), are held in upmarket restaurants. The dinners will have equal numbers of men and women, about 30 at an event. They also arrange for other social events such as trips to the opera, concerts, theatre and art galleries, or to the big fun sporting events such as Henley, Royal Ascot and Wimbledon. The organisations also host big black-tie dinner dances, balls and Valentine's or New Year's parties.

You pay to join the network and also for each event, but everyone is pre-screened and you can guarantee that they will be normal, attractive and intelligent people from the urban professions. This way, you're leaving less to chance and fate, trying to narrow down some of the options. It's unlikely you'd be a member for many years. But for a short time, such membership can widen your social circle and might bring you lots of new friends and acquaintances, or a new partner.

If you are exceedingly cash-rich and even more time-starved, then there is also an organisation set up to meet your needs. It advertises in upscale newspapers, with the small print declaring that a potential member must have over £1million in liquid assets. Whether it insists on women members being quite so well-endowed in a fiscal way is not altogether clear. But gentlemen must have the bucks, and the clout, to be accepted on its books.

There is obviously a need for such an exclusive '**personalised match-making**, partner head-hunting and lifestyle service', as it seems to be attracting plenty of publicity. Such agencies go out of their way to identify or head-hunt suitable men and women using a variety of sources, including using the 'personal ads' in the major quality newspapers such as the *Daily Telegraph*, *The Times* and *Financial Times* as a teaser to find new clients. They will also attend business networking events, social and private member clubs. Or they might send their head-hunter to clubs and glamorous functions looking for potential husbands and wives for wealthy clients.

Smaller bespoke introduction agencies are also beginning to emerge as new niche markets in what might be considered a crowded field. Obviously with so many cash-rich and time-poor professionals out there in the marketplace, the same people who invent new businesses as 'butlers' or 'life coaches' are now offering to help the busy exec not only to find a date, but also to arrange the restaurant, fix up a weekend away and order the flowers. Today's businessman tends to be a world traveller, devoting more time to aeroplanes and hotels than to his sofa and little black book. It's hardly surprising that he may find the search for a compatible lifetime partner a daunting prospect.

That being said, an awful lot of people will have signed up to an internet dating site, or more than one, as well as pursuing offline dating events. Many of the larger and more established internet sites also **host functions** and events to bring their members together. These might include early evening drinks, or huge dinners held in hotels, or smaller activity-related events. I attended one of the latter, a cookery evening on Valentine's night: the most notorious evening on the singles' calendar (although it ties with New Year's Eve) in bringing out the misery, despair and 'what can I do about my life' anguish for those not in firm partnerships. The sight of all those balloons, red hearts, chocolates, flowers and expensive meals for two in restaurants that won't take bookings if you're not a couple, is enough to leave the sanest feeling weak at the knees.

Hosted by the pan-European internet dating site, Parship, at Leith's Cookery School in Kensington, about 30 men and another 30 women met to enjoy wine and socialising, before the rather forbidding task of putting together a three-course meal under the tutelage of the Leith's chefs and assistants. They were grouped in fours, ready to move around the cooking benches between course preparation, so they all got to meet and mingle. Not a Gordon Ramsay f*** word in earshot.

Most were having a great time, but several did confess that they found it nerve-racking or terrifying, reinforcing my view that putting yourself back out on the singles scene can be very difficult for those who are may be shy, reticent or battle-scarred from a previous relationship, or just emerging from a long marriage, sticky divorce, or the shock of sudden widowhood.

They don't sound too cheerful as a bunch, but then it was Valentine's night, which focuses the mind. I felt, however, that they represent a good cross-section of the kind of people who are on the dating scene from their mid-30s to mid-50s.

• • • • • • • • • • •

'Sometimes I just think the solitary life might be best.'

Laura: *I can't tell you how terrifying I find this whole experience. I was with my husband for 35 years after we met at 17. I've now been separated for two years and the divorce went through a few months ago. I've really never been on the dating scene ever at all. My children are grown, though one is still at university. My husband has bought me out of our business, so I'm OK financially. All my friends are married and happily so. I joined the Parship site recently and have been emailing someone who I'm about to meet on Saturday night. I think it's going to be tough going for me!*

Simon: *My wife died five years ago and since then I've concentrated on my career and bringing up the children. But they're getting older now so I decided it was time to try something else. I'm not sure about the matches you are shown on the online dating sites. Sometimes I just think the solitary life might be best.*

Peter: *I'm a widower trying to work out how to get back into life again, after three years on my own. I've been fairly active on the online site and have met a few people. But I do find it time-consuming if you work the whole site properly. I've had several dates with one woman, but she's not sure about me right now, so I thought that rather than stay at home on my own, as I enjoy cooking this would be a good way to get out.*

Anthea: *I came along with my girlfriend, for a laugh I suppose. I'm 38. Well it was my birthday yesterday and several people forgot about it. So I thought that I have to make more effort to meet new people. I was married to the love of my life for many years and recently went through a painful divorce, so I suppose I haven't been actively looking, just concentrating on my career for a few years. But I put up my profile online last night and felt coming to this could also be a way of getting out and meeting new people – hopefully having some fun too.*

• • • • • • • • • •

The most obvious course of action for someone in your age group, if you've tried internet dating, social events, and everything else going, is to consider paying for a **personal introduction agency**. I say for your age group as they really do have cut-off age ranges of 26–45 (or maybe 47) for women and 30–57 for men. But if you can find the money for the investment (anywhere from £2,000 to £30,000 a year), then as a reasonably short-term financial outgoing it might be the least offensive of ways to go about dating. It is certainly very much a niche market, as the majority of men and women I spoke to felt that dating was expensive enough – and there's a huge amount of people who don't even want to pay for the internet sites that charge a fee – but at the same time you are paying for someone else's expertise, experience at matching, and also their own contacts and ability to source new potential partners.

When I began writing this book, I imagined that the by now seemingly old-fashioned introduction agencies would be well and truly on their knees, as the internet swooped in and took over, surely pushing out of business a rather outdated concept that expected people to pay large amounts of money upfront, with no guaranteed results. But the good agencies, tried and trusted, with strong reputations behind them, have survived and maybe will begin to grow again as more disillusioned-with-online-dating victims find their way to their doors. Many of them also have an internet dating service attached to their name, whereby they can recommend men or women who don't fit the age criteria, who can't afford their fees or who live too far away.

The reason for the early cut-off date for women is that there just aren't enough men in their older years who will sign up and pay to join. Men still want to meet women younger than them, so the 45-plus group of women miss out. It's also true that more women sign up to these agencies than men, largely because they prefer the idea that potential men will have been ID checked and passed. The men who sign up do so because they are very busy and too successful at work, which is in itself a trap. They want to meet an educated and interesting woman who has also been vetted or who will at least be reasonably sane. Busy career-oriented men don't want to run the risk of meeting freeloaders, timewasters or women who might endanger their professional reputation.

●●●●●●●●●●●

'Really I want a mirror image of myself.'

We met Graziella in the previous chapter, with her very strong views on why she would not put herself up on the 'eBay' of internet dating sites. She has only recently embarked on her new role as a client of a personal introduction agency, so her final opinion is still out of court.

I describe it as a service, as opposed to the do-it-yourself method of the internet. And, as a busy person, it saves me an enormous amount of time. Also, in my opinion if a man pays an agency, it means he's taken the trouble to go in to be interviewed and reveal personal details to their staff. You know then at least they are serious. The men I've met through the agency are professionals or businessmen, some are self-employed, and all are very nice people. They tend to be reasonably successful, but busy and often travel a lot, so they just don't have time to meet women in the normal way. They don't use the internet because of the time element and privacy aspects. You can't imagine a successful businessman wasting all those hours trawling the net.

Of course I'm looking for a certain amount of income in a man, but the money is not so important as that they are happy and successful in what they do. A man in the mid-40s to early-50s range, someone with children, probably divorced. I prefer men to be fathers as then they are aware of the parental complexities. Really I want a mirror image of myself – someone happy in themselves, successful, ambitious enough to pursue their career.

Will I continue with the agency if my year's payment doesn't produce anyone suitable? I don't know. I still couldn't imagine turning to the internet.

• • • • • • • • • •

What about placing a **personal ad** in one of the quality newspapers? You might think surely these ads have disappeared now that most newspapers have their own internet dating sites. Newspapers are keen to keep the personal ads alive, as they are a valuable source of advertising income. Personal ads are now making leaps and bounds as they link to voicemail for taped messages. For those men and women nervous of exposure on the internet, the personal ads continue to provide a good service and an alternative method of finding potential partners. One hidden benefit of placing an ad is that the headhunters from the personal introduction agencies often trawl these ads searching for likely new candidates for their clients. So you might just find that a suitable man or woman out there is introduced to you from your appealing description in the ad.

Smaller, **market-segmented agencies** are also springing up, as would-be entrepreneurs come up with new schemes to meet perceived demand. One such is operated as a one-man band, introducing British men to Japanese women. Mostly the women live in the United Kingdom and are keen to meet British men, as they have learnt to enjoy a western lifestyle. The man behind the business, Meet Your Future, realised the potential market when he met his own Japanese girlfriend and found little notes slipped his way – 'I would like you to find me nice British man like you' – from her friends and work colleagues. Numbers are small, with about 50 people, equally men and women, for whom he carries out a detailed and careful personalised service.

So you're in the over-50s group

Now you're going to think I'm being mean, ageist and cruel here – just because I don't have a long list of special things for the middling-age group. How could I be, as I'm one of you! But the honest answer is that there aren't a whole host of events organised for this age group, no doubt largely because there just isn't seen to be the potential income to be sourced. The internet has brought new life to the 50-plus group, and that is one great truth. Whereas in the past, widow(er)s, divorce(e)s and just singles once past the prime of youth would have been relegated to the second division, now there is nothing stopping them, and they are reportedly one of the most active age groups involved in internet dating.

My view is that anyone at any age should get involved in all the events, the social networking, the clubs, hobbies that I've been highlighting in this chapter. If one doesn't exist in your neighbourhood, then now is your chance to get out there and start up a new network. There are websites devoted to your age range; there are also established networking groups, dance groups, sporting events and political parties. Groups such as Saga have a 'social networking' arm on their website.

I believe that this is one area desperate for growth. So who is going to be the clever entrepreneur to get up and run with it? Over to you . . .

Let's see whether you think you are the type to benefit most from 'offline' dating methods. Take this quiz.

Quiz

How confident are you?

When it comes to impressing a potential mate, a little confidence goes a long way. But we all have our little insecurities that can get in the way. If you want to create an air of confidence, you can work on it. Confident people are not just born that way, they grow into it. So take this test to work out whether you're super-confident or if there's room for improvement.

1. *Imagine you travel to work on the train every morning. Recently you've spotted someone who's caught your eye. He/she is on the same train most mornings and you've made eye contact but that's all. Would you be able to say hello and start a conversation?*

   a) I'd definitely go for it. Nothing ventured, nothing gained.

b) I'd like to pluck up the courage to speak to him/her. I might be able to if we bumped into each other regularly.

c) I'd smile at him/her and see what happened. If he/she smiled back, I'd try and start up a conversation.

d) I'd love to be able to go up to him/her but I don't think I'd be able to do it.

2. *A good friend has invited you round for a barbeque party. You've made an effort to look nice. A few of your friends are there, but you haven't met most of the people there before. You've been introduced to an attractive and single guy/girl, who works with your friend. What do you do?*

a) I'd blush and pretend to go and find the loo.

b) I'd be polite and chat, but I'd probably find it difficult to relax, let alone flirt with him/her.

c) I'd be myself and wouldn't find it difficult chatting away. I'm not sure whether I'd be able to make it clear that I fancied him/her.

d) I'd enjoy a bit of flirting and banter if he/she was reciprocating but he/she would have to make the first move.

e) I'd flirt and have fun with it. If I thought he/she might fancy me too, then I'd probably suggest we went out on a date.

3. *You've been single for a while and you decide to try internet dating, as a couple of your friends have met people that way. So you've exchanged a few emails with someone and chatted*

on the phone, and so far, so good. You've agreed to meet up for dinner. Assuming everything has gone well so far, how do you think the date will go?

a) I'd hope for the best but really I'd be expecting the worst.

b) I'd be quite nervous but just hope for the best.

c) I'd expect we'd have fun if we had already got on well on the phone, but as for anything else, it would depend a lot upon whether or not he/she fancied me.

d) I'd be confident that he/she would fancy me, but you can't predict the chemistry until you meet in person.

e) I'd like to think we'd have fun, but realistically, I'd be worrying he/she wouldn't fancy me.

4. *Could you ask a colleague out on a date?*

a) Yes. If we were getting on well and both single, I think I could ask him/her out for a drink.

b) I think so, but I would have to have already got the signals that he/she fancied me.

c) I'd chat and flirt with him/her and hope that I didn't have to do the chasing.

d) Unlikely. Even if we were getting on really well, I just couldn't face the rejection at work.

e) No. I'd just be too shy to ask him/her out.

5. *You've got to know a man/woman really well as a friend. You've known him/her for quite a while and you're both*

single. You've realised you've had feelings for him/her for some time. Could you tell him/her how you feel?

a) It just wouldn't happen. If he/she was a friend then I would just ignore any romantic feelings and make them go away as I just wouldn't want to get hurt.

b) I think it's unlikely I'd say anything, as it would just be too embarrassing if he/she didn't feel the same way.

c) I'd go out with him/her and a few friends for a big night out and try to end up snogging him/her.

d) If I really had the hots for him/her I'd definitely say something.

6. *How confident are you that you could approach someone that you found attractive in a bar?*

   a) Very. I'd just go up to him/her and go for it.

   b) Fairly. I'd usually give it a go.

   c) Fairly. I'd make eye contact and smile and then approach him/her.

   d) I'd make eye contact and smile and he/she would usually end up approaching me.

   e) I'd be very shy. I might try to smile but it's unlikely I could go over and chat him/her up.

   f) I wouldn't be able to go up to a stranger.

7. *If you did manage to get chatting to someone in a bar, how confident are you that he/she would be attracted to you, once you'd got past the first few minutes?*

a) Extremely. I think once we get chatting most people find my personality attractive.

b) Very. Most people find me easy to talk to and interesting.

c) Fairly, but you never know who you're going to hit it off with.

d) Not sure. I'm not everyone's cup of tea.

e) Not very confident.

8. *Based on your appearance, how confident are you that other people will find you attractive if you're at a party?*

a) Extremely. I'm told I'm very attractive.

b) Very. People say I'm attractive but everyone has different taste.

c) Fairly. I think I'd appeal to a few people.

d) Not so sure. I like to think that I might appeal to someone, but this doesn't happen often.

e) Not very. I'd have to rely more on my personality.

9. *Imagine you've gone on a first date with someone. It has gone well and you think he/she fancied you. Would you be able to phone him/her and suggest another date?*

a) I would do it if I had to, but I'd prefer it if it wasn't down to me.

b) I'd have no problem with it. If I was keen, then I'd go for it.

c) I'd be a bit nervous about it, but I'd do it anyway.

d) I'd wait for him/her to call me.

Your answers

1. a) 4 b) 2 c) 1 d) 0
2. a) 0 b) 0 c) 1 d) 2 e) 4
3. a) 0 b) 1 c) 2 d) 4 e) 2
4. a) 4 b) 3 c) 2 d) 1 e) 0
5. a) 0 b) 1 c) 3 d) 4
6. a) 4 b) 3 c) 2 d) 3 e) 1 f) 0
7. a) 4 b) 3 c) 2 d) 1 e) 0
8. a) 4 b) 3 c) 2 d) 1 e) 0
9. a) 2 b) 4 c) 3 d) 0

Scoring

Has it all gone to your head? (32–36)

You're certainly not lacking in confidence! If you've already found the love of your life, then this may not be a problem. If you're still single, then take note: whilst confidence can be a great turn-on, you need to be careful to temper this with warmth and sensitivity. It's great that you can approach people you fancy and flirt with such ease. But if you're this confident you can afford to be more selective. If you're trying to impress someone, you don't want him or her to end up feeling that you're doing this sort of thing every day. Don't just chat up anyone and everyone just because you can, and when you do get chatting to people that you find attractive, don't be afraid to show a little bit of vulnerability from time to time. It can be endearing and shows that you're not being too pushy.

Confident, but not arrogant (8–31)

When it comes to confidence, you seem to have struck the right balance. Your confidence is one of your biggest strengths, and if you can work with this, you will come across as naturally charismatic. Everyone has feelings of insecurity and shyness at times. The difference is that some people have it at the forefront of their minds and this stops them from being perceived how they want to be. Other people hide their insecurity so well that they can appear arrogant or pushy. You don't tend to do either of these, so you'll come across as confident, but not big-headed.

Too shy to try (0–7)

No one feels 100 per cent confident all of the time, but your shyness could be holding you back from meeting someone and having a great relationship. There's no need to change your personality: you don't need to become some sort of womaniser/man-eater. But why not try making eye contact and smiling more? If you can relax and chat to men/women on a daily basis and just have a laugh and maybe flirt a bit, then when you do meet someone you fancy, it shouldn't be such a daunting prospect just to smile and start up a conversation.

One small thing you could do is start giving more compliments (provided they're sincere) to both men and women. Try telling someone you like their necklace or their shoes for example. And if you still can't get past your shyness, you could try enrolling on an evening course. It might be nerve-racking, but that's the best way to conquer your fears, just like facing a phobia. Chat to people you meet, but just tell yourself you're not looking for anything romantic – you're just going to be friendly in order to increase your confidence. Then why not try internet dating? It's much easier to approach people this way, and you can exchange a few emails before you even meet, so it's not like you have to start from nothing.

If you do arrange a date, be yourself and practise positive and confident body language, even if you don't feel it. That way you know you can always appear confident outwardly, no matter how you feel.

Chapter 5

Getting to the First Date

Now we've looked into the various methods of finding a date, reasons you might be finding this situation stressful, and how to go about sourcing a really good, compatible match. It's time to move on and look at how best to progress from the world of idle chat, flirtation, emails, phone calls and text messages, to the real-life actual meet-in-the-flesh date.

If you've chosen the path of online dating sites, you will of course first have to put up your profile and photo. If you're the type who is happier going to singles social events, speed dating, joining a singles group or network – or simply scouring the streets and subways for someone who sparks your fancy – then you won't need to put pen to paper or fingers to keyboard. But I'd suggest it's a good idea to write that profile anyway. It will force you to think about yourself, who you really are, what are your best attributes and what sort of person you're looking for. It might mean you give up an evening to scribble some notes and then try them out on a friend to hear his or her comments or reactions. If the instantaneous answer is, 'Don't be so reticent. You're a lot more interesting than that. What about the time you did so and so . . . ?' then listen to the feedback and determine to be more bold and forthcoming. If you've had to revamp your CV in recent times, that's also a very good training ground for rethinking how to promote yourself in the best possible light.

Writing a profile that will be appealing and attractive

Are you squirming in your chair right now, at the very thought of having to put pen to paper and write about yourself? Don't worry, it's not the easiest chore for anyone. As with any form of self-promotion, there's a fine line between over selling and being too shy or not wishing to come over as someone with massive amounts of self-confidence. Self-deprecation is a very common trait and it can work if the humour comes across, though sometimes it misfires and will make you sound like a miserable old so-and-so.

One trick that many people adopt is to browse the various online sites first to see who is up there, the different types of men or women, and what they are saying about themselves. Also you need to do this background research to check on which site you feel most comfortable with, and on which you see the most men or women that might appeal to you.

One other piece of research I imagine many people do is to enter the site as a test, in the guise of someone of the opposite gender, putting in desired age range and location, and seeing what their immediate competition: a) looks like, and b) how they describe themselves.

Big warning: be very careful not to plagiarise someone else's profile. This does occasionally take place, and the victim of the plagiarised profile will rightly be very upset and may ask the operators to have your profile taken down. How will they ever know, you might ask? Because the same kind of men or women will be reading your profile as theirs, and may mention that it looks very similar. They will know whose original writing it all is!

On the less controlled sites it's been discovered that some profiles are fakes, but if you pay to join one of the more reputable online sites it's unlikely you will come across such time-wasters, as part of the cost you pay is spent on policing the entries, reading the text sent in for profiles, checking the photo isn't the same one being used on other sites, and that the details of the applicant match his or her credit card. You can read more about the better-known scams in Chapter 7.

If you sign up to the free sites, however, you might just have to take the outcome of such fraudulent behaviour with a pinch of salt. Many people use quick deceptive stunts for fairly reasonable motives. For example, one man told me he put up a false profile and photo pretending to be a woman seeking other women. He just wanted to see what lesbian women wrote about themselves and how they communicated, compared with the heterosexual women he had come across online. The difference was quite startling. Lesbian women promote themselves much more openly as sexual partners. They responded to (his) her profile very quickly, quite blatantly looking for sex. Their photos, too, he says were much more upfront. In the end, feeling uncomfortable with these revelations, he took down this fake profile.

What to say in your profile

Make sure you are positive and upbeat, show where your passions lie (but not in terms of sex, unless that is your main goal). You should aim to be interesting and different, without being so wacky that you come across as something of a nutcase. Avoid clichés, and also try hard not to sound too intense, emotional or overly deep. These traits can be very off-putting. If you read samples of women's profiles on several sites, you'll find those who talk about their fear of rejection and how they 'love sitting by the fireside holding hands'. That sort of tone might be deliberate, in that they want to put off potential point-scorers on the sexual front. But the rather old-fashioned image can also be off-putting to a man. Similarly, men often indulge in anti-female rants along the lines of 'not interested in any more women who'll see me as a free meal'. Don't talk about how men or women in the past have hurt you, or reveal your emotional sensitivity too easily.

Think about something unusual you have done or that will really pique someone's interest. This is a piece of writing, and as such, it should leap off the page as it would in a good novel or film script.

If you are looking for a serious relationship and are paying to find that compatible partner, then do be honest about the important things: your age, your height, your weight, whether you smoke or not, are in work, are reasonably solvent, have or want children. However you can be vague about your desire to have children, if you feel that might be off-putting.

When Maddy was writing her profile she looked into some of the other women's profiles on her chosen site, to see what they were saying about themselves:

> *The popular women all seemed to be tall, lanky, long-haired and white. There was no one with short hair (like mine) in the top 20. I'm always honest, and in my profile wrote that I'm quite 'geeky' and can also be seen as blokey in my mannerisms. I said that I find both David Bowie and Johnny Depp sexy. I also wrote, 'Baby-eating anarchists are welcome.' I got a few responses at first, not the deluge that more obviously attractive and amenable women probably receive. And there was no one I really felt 'phwoar' about.*

What kind of photo to post up on the site

There's no way round the unfortunate truth that we (both men and women) do tend to judge people first on their photos – the profile comes second. That's no different from meeting people in a more organic way. You will only start to talk to the chap at the bar or in the supermarket if you find him remotely attractive.

Men are more blatant about the fact that they rely primarily on the photo as the method of selection, even if, as Chris said earlier, they worry about not being sure what type of looks they find really appealing. In previous case studies we have read that most of the men said their initial impression of the woman was that they liked her photo. The women tend not to be so proscriptive about the initial photo, and are willing to give someone the benefit of the doubt if he writes interestingly and sounds fun or nice.

So, if as a woman you're going to put up a photo on an online site and you are worried about how photogenic you appear, then it's worth having a good photo taken, by either a friend or a professional photographer. You need to find a quirky angle that gives the best impression. Don't look too suggestive or rely solely on your built-up cleavage as a way of luring the men – unless you are simply out to get lots of sex without strings, that is. At the same time, don't hide your best features in a prim, school ma'am-ish way. You need to look warm, happy, interested, fun to be with and energetic; sexually alive without looking overly sexed-up. I'm amazed at how many women will pay to join a specific site and then just take a picture of themselves at home with a camera or mobile phone, and wonder why they get very few contacts. If you're young, still in your prime and know that you come across well to strangers, then maybe you can afford to sit back and relax. For anyone else, you will reap what you sow in terms of the effort you put in.

Now having said that about women and their photos, let me make a big plea to men. You too should spend time making sure your photo makes you look appealing, fun, interested (and interesting) and as good-looking as you can manage. It's amazing how many men seem to pay the photo little regard, obviously reflecting the view that looks aren't important in a woman's choice of men. But looks are important. And few women are going to be turned on by a man who has let his looks and physique sag, so that his hair is wild and untamed, his beard looks like it could do with a maintenance check-up, his clothes are unkempt and he can't even be bothered to take a good, sharp, professional-quality digital photo.

Don't use a photo in which you've obviously cut out the previous girlfriend, or use one that includes your teenage daughter, hoping that her prettiness will rub off on you. Also don't run with that snapshot of yourself on the beach last summer, where the beer bottles are all too obvious. If your girth is getting in the way, then don't flatter yourself by using a ten-year-old picture when you had a six-pack.

Men or women – don't put up a photo of yourself naked, or semi-naked. If you do this on one of the better, paid-for sites it will probably be taken down. If you decide to sell yourself that way, then you know what sort of clients you will attract!

Posting up digital jpegs is relatively easy these days. But if you just are so non-IT minded, you can always send the operators your print in the post.

What to do next

Your profile and photo are posted up, you've been to speed dating or a social event, and you've managed to gather some people interested in you. Who makes the first contact, man or woman?

As with anything else in today's world, the normal traditional boundaries have gone. The game is open to both parties. However, that being said, it is true that once over the age of about 35–40, the majority of women still claim they prefer to have the initial contact made by a man – even if it's just for him to flag that he's interested. Most dating websites have 'flirts' or 'whispers' or 'favourites' or 'fans', which is a way of saying an early 'here's looking at you' before anything else transpires. Some men or women will not even answer those in detail, but merely reply in kind or send a stock 'icebreaker' line back.

As a woman, if you have paid to be on an online dating site, it really is worth breaking your own rules and making some early contacts yourself. Spend some time browsing through all the available men, and make lists of whom you might contact. It can be time-consuming, but you will get more out of your membership if you are an active participant. If you're too quiet, sitting at the back of the class, men will either think you're not very lively, too shy, or that you've met someone and just not bothered to take down your profile.

When do you write your first real email?

Maddy describes her early days on a paid-for online dating site:

I wrote first to my number one match and we got on well online. When we met up, we got on well enough and had about three dates. We made each other laugh, but really there was no spark at all in that three-week period, so I gave him up.

By then I'd spotted James who had just signed up. He's white, my age, tall at 6 ft 2 in [1.88 m]. He writes and edits as a freelancer. His last long-term relationship also ended three years ago, and he was looking to meet someone to stay with, maybe have kids. His profile made me laugh, it was all about his travels and adventures, where a lot of the guys' profiles seem affected. I suppose that's understandable if they're trying to sell themselves to get a date. In his profile he admits that he's quite shy and certainly not the type to march up to a woman in a bar with chat-up lines. Basically, I thought he looked very sexy.

She took the first step, not only writing the first email but also pushing for an early date:

I initiated the email and wrote to him at length. He took a couple of days to reply, which worried me, but then he wrote back an equally long email, which was funny and witty. Before James, I'd have had a few weeks' correspondence leading up to a meeting. The main downside to internet dating is that however honest they might have been in their profile, they're still different from what you imagined. I didn't want to go through that process this time and felt it better to meet quickly just to see if there was a spark. I wasn't going to waste time with the fantasies again.

How long to keep up with the email or phone communication

My advice would normally be, as in Maddy's case, to keep the emailing short and sweet: make sure you meet quite early on, so you don't waste too much time in the 'aren't we getting on well on email' phase, which as I've said earlier can come to a crushing, bitter end which you actually meet. There are times, as many of the stories in this book prove, that being forced into a lengthy email correspondence, with phone calls and even texts, can be a successful slow-burn in a lead up to genuine romance.

Here's Mary Ann, the young Australian PR executive living in London, whose whole group of friends uses online internet dating sites:

> *When Sam and I first got in touch, we were emailing for about three months. I was going out with someone else and so was he. In his profile, he describes himself as shy. He's also like a big giant. He wrote on the site: 'If you don't like big guys, then stop reading now.' But I was feeling cowed by his being so big and tall. In the end, I finally persuaded him to meet me. Turns out he was working in a street a block away from where I live. We'd even bumped into each other at a music festival!*

Kathy and Mark were also forced to take time before they met, as she was still living in Paris while he worked in London. Here's how she wrote her profile, which was found by Mark:

My profile said 'I'm a Eurostar girl who can mend her own punctures.' I came across as very independent. I was very choosy in my profile and search criteria. I knew I don't fancy men shorter than me and I'm quite tall at 5 ft 10 in [1.77 m]. And I tend to like men with dark hair.

Mark says he really liked my photo and was immediately physically attracted to me. But his photo didn't have that 'wow' factor for me. I grew to like him from what I found out. From when he first made contact, there were a few months to go before I would move back, and that time gave us space to get to know each other slowly and to be more romantic. We'd write poems to each other by text. I'd come into the office and there'd be a lovely email from him.

She met up with a couple of other men who'd also emailed her in the first few days, just so she could check out that she wasn't getting too carried away by a fantasy about Mark.

For Sally and Jason, while he was still in Edinburgh and she was in Leeds, they couldn't meet up for three weeks. Once again this distancing effect proved a success:

We talked on the phone and emailed each other a lot. I was still quite nervous of meeting anyone at that time. Then it was Valentine's Day and he sent me an e-card. He was going to be in Leeds soon, so we just waited and talked a lot on the phone. He sounded nice and I began to let myself believe he must be a genuinely nice guy. Then when we did meet, it was so easy, as though we knew each other, because we'd already found out so much about each other.

But perhaps the ultimate in not meeting up quickly took place in the case of Jenni and Tom. If ever you feel the path to true love should run smooth, then take heart from their story. Every obstacle possible seemed to come in their way before they actually met up several months later:

> *I met about five men from the site apart from Tom. But they weren't going anywhere. One was sweet, because when he came to our date, he'd made a minidisk of flamenco music for me. But in the meantime I was getting emails from Tom, who came across as intelligent and entertaining. Neither of us pushed for an early meeting. I was always busy and we lived at opposite ends of London. Towards the end of the summer, he did suggest meeting up. I was intrigued that he'd persevered with our email correspondence, so I wrote back saying 'You name the date, place and time.'*
>
> *That was on the Thursday. The following Monday I broke my back in an accident that took place on a company day out, on a jet-ski. Holed up in a hospital bed on the south coast I couldn't even go online for two months. That was a terrible time for me, as you can imagine. It's fortunate that I'm good at denial, as it never really occurred to me I might never walk again. I do recall feeling bad about this chap who had fixed a date with me. Maybe he'd gone to meet me and thought I'd stood him up? When I could finally sit up in bed and got hold of a laptop, I saw his return email suggesting we meet that Tuesday at the London Aquarium. Of course, I'd never even replied to it. I really had to pluck up courage to write him with my 'good excuse'.*

He took some time to believe me – well, it does sound like the tallest of stories, doesn't it? When he didn't get a reply to the email, it seems he just gave up on me, so at least he hadn't gone there and hung about waiting, getting mad at being stood up.

I was able to send him a photo of me being winched up to the helicopter and also from the thank you party I gave for the Royal National Lifeboat Institution men, without whom I'd have been paralysed for life. He came round then and suggested we try meeting again. But now, I had to explain that although I could walk, there was no way I could manage the trek from my flat to a restaurant unaccompanied. He'd have to come to my place and I'd have to perch on a barstool. The timing for his going to Australia was getting closer, so the odds were completely stacked against anything happening between us.

They did meet and immediately hit it off. As you have read in previous chapters, Jenni and Tom fell in love with each other quickly, and it was decided that they would apply together for emigration to Australia on a partner visa. The delays that cropped up in his application process gave them the necessary time together. As it happens, they went to visit Melbourne, his chosen site for immigration, this New Year. Tom proposed, and now they'll be travelling out there as a married couple!

Getting to the first date

Reading the story above, it makes you realise that no one can ever be too prescriptive as to what might be a good or bad sign. We can only imagine Tom's confusion when this young woman he had already set his mind on failed to follow up on the initial email for a first date. But such disappointments can be quite common in both the online and offline world. The more normal reason behind her coldness would have been a sad coincidence whereby she met someone else the night before and decided to continue dating that person. It would have been polite for her to have emailed the reason, but we can forgive her in these circumstances. Besides, they did not really know each other, except from a few emails.

The story illustrates that point very clearly – you don't know each other when you first arrange to meet, so do be careful to cover all bases. Make sure you exchange mobile phone numbers, as the person may not be instantly recognisable from his or her photo. Also make sure you arrange to meet in a popular, fairly busy, public place. Never agree to meet in someone's flat or office, where you have no easy escape route if things turn difficult.

If you've met your prospective date online, you will probably have exchanged a few emails and even emailed off the site, so you'll have exchanged personal email addresses first. Some people have their own websites or blogs, so you can begin to find out more information about each other. If you feel the person is trustworthy, then there is no reason not to give out your real name – though you are under no obligation to provide that information before you have met, if you wish to keep it secret. There are people who will immediately run a Google search on your name, so be careful if you'd rather that didn't take place. There are also people who will do other searches to find where you live. If you get a hint from a potential date that he/she is doing that, my advice would be to stop corresponding with that person immediately. Paranoid or obsessive behaviour, if it shows up so early in your communications, can only get worse and might be the clue to a very dark side to the person's personality.

Many people choose the normal crowded bars and restaurants as a good 'safe' place to meet. Others might prefer somewhere safe and potentially interesting like an art gallery that has a café or restaurant. On a summer's eve, a wine bar with tables outside is a nice venue; or along a riverside, where there are usually pubs and space to go for a short walk.

I personally wouldn't get involved in being invited to go to the cinema, or for dinner, with someone you've never met and don't know at all (despite his or her supposed wit and intelligence on email). If you don't live near each other, then both of you will have to drive or travel to meet halfway. One of you could take a train to the other's nearby city. But be warned, such journeys can seem like an awful investment of time and money if there is no spark between the two of you.

It's not only women who might find themselves compromised. I've talked to men who were quite shocked to discover that the hotel coffee shop recommended by a woman as a suitable meeting place outside of town is then used as the groundwork for 'Shall we move to one of the rooms?' Some men, as well as women, can feel decidedly put-upon if sex is suggested as the natural next move after a shared cup of coffee or glass of wine! If that's not what you want, you're under no obligation to get involved. Just make your excuses and leave, sharpish.

Who should suggest where to meet

In discussing this, the same holds true for two people who have met online, through speed dating, at a singles social event, or who have been brought together through a personal introduction agency.

Quite often the person who initiates the date will have a location in mind. At other times, however, you can feel the clanking machinery of a relationship already beginning to go wrong, when neither makes a bold move over where to meet. Surely he should be the one to lead, she thinks. Why can't she just come up with a suggestion, I get tired of always making these decisions, he thinks. If the man doesn't immediately suggest something that appeals, then it's probably better for the woman to come up with the idea. That way she will feel more comfortable about the meeting place, and that can make her less vulnerable.

Graziella, who is meeting men through an introduction agency, shows that many of the issues are just the same when it comes to the actual first meeting or 'date':

> *When your meeting has been set up through the agency, unlike the internet dating sites, you don't always know what they look like. In this agency, they don't show you the photo of the man. But you have been told a little of their background. The first meeting is meant to be very quick, just a drink at a bar, a short taster. It's*

best to wait for the dinner date till next time. It's also better to meet quickly, so you don't have a chance to build up a fantasy about them.

What to talk about

It may sound silly, but this is a very important issue. Sometimes, it's more a question of what not to talk about. For men and women who are in the second round of marriage, after divorce, or separation after some time living together, the real problem is in holding back from talking about those years and the problems you faced or are still going through.

Here are some handy tips on what to choose:

- Look over the profile or the notes made on you by an agency, and think of some light questions you can ask about their interests.
- It is also a good idea to think of some interesting stories to tell about what you have been doing recently.
- Do you have a special interest or hobby? If so, try to focus on some fascinating side that would appeal to an outsider.
- Where did you last go on holiday? Is there something significant to say about that trip?
- Last weekend, this coming weekend, what sort of things do you like to do?
- Your children – some funny little story about life with the kids.
- Your home or flat: are you into home décor or renovations?

- Sport: do you take part in any sport or related activity?
- Your job or colleagues: some light-hearted tale about your working day.

And these are the topics to avoid:

- Don't grill your new 'date' about his/her life, salary, cars, amount spent on holidays, as though you were running an investigation into him/her.
- Don't moan about your ex, the custody battles, your earnings, your pension, how your former husband or wife mistreated you.
- Don't start to rant with barely disguised anger about how awful you think men are (women), or that women are just out to fleece men and treat them as meal tickets (men).
- Don't get into a morbid discussion about the problems you're having with the children.
- Don't whinge about your job and complain bitterly about your boss or the hours you work.
- Don't discuss your therapist and what he/she says about you.
- Don't go on too much about all the alternative medicines you take.
- Don't talk excessively about your children and how well they're doing at school, in drama classes or at university (or how badly).
- Don't say you're desperate to have a baby.

- Don't say you're desperate to meet someone to make your life better.
- Don't crack too many jokes and expect them to be laughed at.
- Don't laugh too loud or shrilly (women), or raucously (men).
- Don't be too flirtatious, smiling or laughing madly, as though desperate to appear like the most with-it person in the room.
- Don't talk in a monologue, not letting the other person get a word in edgeways.

Social discourse, light conversation, is a surprisingly difficult art, which the majority of us probably find quite stressful. It's often easier to be the so-called 'interviewer', as this would appear to give you the upper hand. You are the one who leads off with the questions, so you can fill the awkward silences. But that may not make your partner feel very comfortable. Or, you might find that both of you are rather quiet and retiring, so conversation is stilted and never flows well.

The main trap to this kind of meeting, I find, is that one or the other will set off the conversation by asking 'So why are you on this site/looking for a date/a member of the agency?' It's a sort of 'So tell me what brings you to this point in your life?' leading question that can catch you out unawares, as you start to reveal far too much of the inner truth. The trap having been set, the unwitting victim then lets him or herself get totally embroiled in what can lead to a long rambling whine. 'I'm so miserable, my life's been such a mess' – and the whole potential relationship can dissolve in the first 30 minutes.

Similarly, if you have phone conversations before you actually meet, don't let them meander off down one of the blind alleys listed above. You don't want to talk for too long on the phone, as exactly the same kind of trap can be set and you might go off on a depressive route without realising it. Keep the tone and subject matter reasonably light and upbeat.

What's best to wear

It's fairly normal these days to be casual rather than formal in your dress sense, with a leaning towards 'smart casual'. Women are probably wisest not to turn up on the first date in jeans and flat boots, unless that is the image they have portrayed in the photo on the site and it fits with their overall lifestyle philosophy. If you meet straight from the office, your clothes will probably reflect where you fit in the world right now, but equally an overly severe suit, crisp shirt and smart black court shoes might be rather off-putting to a man who has come to meet you in ordinary trousers with a casual sweater draped charmingly over his shoulders.

Men should make an effort to ensure their shirt is ironed (amazing how many men don't realise that the first thing a woman will notice is a crumpled shirt). If you've never got round to doing your own ironing, then don't wear a shirt, but stick to a casual polo or rugby shirt. Don't turn up to meet a woman in a posh bar or restaurant in unkempt jeans, an unwashed T-shirt or a rather raggy looking windcheater.

For both men and women, even if you're feeling daunted and threatened by this meeting with a stranger, wear clothes that are attractive and make you feel good. They don't have to be brand-new, but they should appear newly washed or pressed, and give an idea of your sort of style.

For women, if you were brown-haired in your photo, and you've now gone blonde, it's best to forewarn him. Also if your photo really does show you with a lot fewer pounds than is the current reality, you might want to mention it lightly in passing before meeting. Unless you are in your mid-20s, don't turn up to a first date in anything too revealing, on the upper or lower half of your body. There's not much point in selling your ample cleavage or trim thighs too overtly, unless you're only after a quick one-night stand.

●●●●●●●●●●

'I was getting slightly drunk and soaking wet.'

People do have first dates where things don't go according to plan, but if destiny is on their side, just as with Jenni and Tom before, it can all progress despite some setbacks along the way. Here's more of Maddy and James' quite incredible story:

Maddy: *I can't say things started off well for us. We agreed on a first date quite quickly, to meet for a drink in central London, late on a Saturday afternoon. Normally*

I'd dress up a bit before such a date. But, earlier in the day, I'd met up with a friend to go on a demonstration and it began pouring with rain. We were out on the streets with a bottle of wine, and I was getting slightly drunk and soaking wet, wearing jeans, which became absolutely sodden.

I remember thinking 'Damn, I've got to go on a date now.' Whether he found it less intimidating that I turned up like that I don't know, but we just got on ridiculously well and immediately felt comfortable with each other. We had drinks, then went for dinner. As we were near my flat in Holborn, I wanted to invite him in so we could continue having a drink and talking, because it was getting late. I said, 'This is not an invitation to come back for sex, but if you want we can go to my place and have another drink.' I sent him home at 5 am and we did just stay up talking.

• • • • • • • • • • •

How to control your nerves before meeting

If you're the type of person who feels very nervous at having to put yourself in a situation where you're going to meet a more or less complete stranger, so that you clam up, your hands start to sweat, your nervous twitch returns, or your chest and neck flush bright red, then you need to concentrate on doing some breathing exercises to overcome this fear. Also remind yourself of the reality of the situation. This is not a job interview. You are not taking to the stage in a West End play. Your life does not depend on your performance. It's just a date, one of hundreds of thousands taking place all around you.

If you've previously met at speed dating, or through some singles social event, you will already have talked about a few things (even if for only three minutes), and that should give you the icebreaker moment to get things rolling again. If you've been matched by a personal introduction agency, you will have read a brief background description, rather similar to a profile that gets posted on an internet dating site, and that should give you plenty to go on to begin the conversation. If you've read about each other on an internet site, have exchanged emails, maybe spoken a couple of times on the phone, and now you're meeting, you already know quite a lot about each other and can always make an icebreaker joke about the person's interest in politics, sport or needlework.

Nervousness can lead us to sometimes clam up and feel we have nothing to say. Or turn too talkative, so that we prattle away about anything, trying to cover up that we don't know how to make a real good conversation. If you find yourself in either of those situations, it's best to be honest at a certain point in the date and apologise, with a laugh, 'Sorry, I tend to talk too much when I'm nervous. It's your turn now.' Or, 'You must think I'm really quiet as I haven't said anything. I'm not usually like this; I just became so nervous when setting out on the date. I'll warm up later, if you'll forgive me this once!' Shyness and nervousness can be charming. We don't all want to meet Mr or Ms Superhuman – in fact most of us really don't want to be faced with a supreme form of human being, or we'd feel even more threatened.

So breathe deeply. Count quietly to 20. Tell yourself you're doing fine, this person wanted to meet you and so you can't be all that bad. Go and wash your hands in the cloakroom, if you feel you're getting sweaty. If you flush easily, then wear a high-necked top or drape a scarf or stole round your shoulders. Watch out for body language that might be off-putting:

- Try to make eye contact. If your eyes wander all over the room, he/she will think either you're not interested in him/her or that you're slightly crazy.
- Don't put your hand over your mouth or sit with your head cupped in your hand, as it will show up your anxiety and nervousness.
- Don't sit back with your hands behind your head, a more male form of behaviour, as it will make you look too casual as though you're not interested in the woman you've invited on the date.
- Don't twiddle your hair, or keep moving a piece of hair around, or even worse, get your comb out in front of the date to tidy up your hairdo. These are all rather obvious signs of nervousness.
- Don't keep your fingers in your mouth, or on your lips, or bite your nails. These are obvious signs of anxiety.
- Don't jingle keys or coins in your pocket, another male behaviour. It makes you seem rushed and ready to leave, another sign of anxiety.

- Don't sit with your arms folded. That's a way of distancing yourself from the date, as though you're not at all interested.

It's not that we can all make ourselves perfect overnight, but signing up to a personal introduction agency does mean you'll get feedback from the agency counsellors about how your dates have gone and what the comments are about you.

As Graziella said of her experience so far:

Dating of any kind is tiring. You're playing games, putting on a flirtatious front, when you might not feel like that. I tend to play it over-cool because I don't want to show that I might be attracted. We get feedback from the agency, after our first dates, and one man commented that I was 'so cool, almost to the point of being distant'.

I think I come over as intimidating. I enjoy a good lifestyle and with my children go on lots of holidays, either skiing or to hot sunny beaches. Maybe I seem too much for the average man. I'm fairly confident by nature, but I come over as unapproachable. I find it hard to work out what men are looking for. Despite the fact most men say they're looking for someone independent, when it comes down to it, they want to be the saviour and knight in shining armour.

Now it's time to take another quiz, on your first-date style.

Quiz

What's your first-date style: predictable or adventurous?

It's vital to create a great impression on a first date. You may have all the chat-up lines and flirting techniques, but would you be guilty of going to the same restaurant on a first date that you've been to countless times before? Would you be willing to go the extra mile to impress and are you brave enough to arrange something a bit different? Take this test to find out.

1. *In terms of looks and personality, would you say you have a 'type' that you tend to go for?*
   a) Yes. I know what I like and I'm sticking to it.
   b) There are certain characteristics that I'm always drawn to but it's not clear-cut.
   c) Some of my exes have been similar but not invariably so, and I'm always open to new possibilities.
   d) I haven't got a type. Sometimes I go from one extreme to another.

2. *Imagine you've met someone who's new at work. Your friends would say he/she was completely unsuitable for you, and you're inclined to agree, but you still think he/she's cute. If he/she asked you on a date would you go?*
   a) Yes definitely – what's there to lose?
   b) I'd be drawn to him/her precisely because he/she was different.

c) I'd be a bit hesitant but I might give in if he/she caught me in the right mood.

d) Very unlikely. If there was a very big age gap and I felt we didn't have much in common then what's the point?

e) Definitely not. If it's never going to be a long-term relationship, why waste my time?

3. *Imagine you've met a great guy/girl at your friend's party. You really hit it off and you've got a good feeling about it. Since then you've been texting and spoken on the phone a couple of times. You've arranged to meet up for your first proper date. Which of the following would you be most likely to do?*

a) Go out for dinner to a nice bistro.

b) Go to the cinema.

c) Go for a trip on the London Eye.

d) Meet for lunch.

e) Go for a coffee.

4. *On your first trip to the cinema, what sort of film would you be most likely to see?*

a) A romantic comedy.

b) Something funny that would make us both laugh.

c) The latest James Bond film.

d) A horror film.

e) A thriller.

f) Something with action, fighting and lots of blood.

g) A costume drama.

h) Something arty.

5. *Your date suggests going bungee jumping. Assuming you're fit enough, would you do it?*

a) Yes. I'd definitely be up for it.

b) I'd think he/she must have a screw loose. Why would we want to do that as a first date?

c) I'd be intrigued but I'd probably say I'd rather leave the bungee jumping until another date, if there is one.

d) He/she would have to cajole me but I could be persuaded.

6. *If left to your own devices to plan a first date, what would you do?*

a) I'd end up saying 'I don't know, what do you want to do?'

b) I'd just think about where was practical for us to meet and then go for a drink or for a meal somewhere that I know.

c) I'd try to go somewhere to eat that I hadn't been to before.

d) I'd go for something interesting that would give us something to talk about, like an exhibition or a trip to the zoo.

e) I'd arrange to go the cinema so at least the silences wouldn't be awkward.

f) I'd plan something active like rollerblading or indoor skiing.

7. *You've been chatting to someone you've met through an internet dating site but he/she doesn't live close by. How far would you be willing to travel out of your way for a first date?*

a) I think my date should travel to me if he/she had asked me out.

b) I'd prefer to stick to a 10-mile radius.

c) I might go up to 50 miles, especially if it meant we went into a city as there would be more choice of things to do.

d) I'd be willing to go to another city altogether, even if it was a few hundred miles away.

e) I'd travel to another country to meet up if I felt there was enough potential.

Your answers

1. a) 0 b) 1 c) 2 d) 4
2. a) 3 b) 4 c)2 d) 1 e) 0
3. a) 0 b) 2 c) 4 d) 0 e) 1
4. a) 0 b) 0 c) 0 d) 4 e) 2 f) 3 g) 1 h) 2
5. a) 4 b) 0 c) 1 d) 3
6. a) 0 b) 0 c) 1 d) 3 e) 1 f) 4
7. a) 0 b) 1 c) 2 d) 3 e) 4

Scoring

Predictable (0–10)

But look on the bright side: at least you know what's expected on a first date and you're following the rules of social etiquette.

You might not be the most exciting date in the world but you probably concentrate on making sure you both feel at ease while you get to know each other better.

Not exactly one of life's risk-takers (11–24)
It's all about calculated risks. You prefer to stick to what's tried and tested but you're always open to new opportunities, as long as they're not too outrageous. You probably know what you like but you'll try something new once in a while. You may well have an adventurous streak but you'd prefer to get to know someone better before straying from the tried and tested first-date formula of drinks, dinner or cinema. Once you've been on a few dates and you're feeling comfortable, you're much more likely to suggest a sporting activity, a picnic or a trip to an exhibition.

Adventurous thrill-seeker (25–28)
No one could accuse you of being boring or predictable. You'd much rather do something a bit different. You want to experience life rather than letting it pass you by. You're open to possibilities and opportunities, and you're not afraid to take a gamble and suggest something unusual for a first date.

Yes or no

So the date is coming to an end – how do you decide whether the two of you want to meet up again? We all need to get used to reading body signals. If the other person is seemingly fidgety or looking bored, if he or she glances at a watch, or keeps picking up a mobile phone as though willing it to ring, you can safely say he or she has had enough of your company. If by comparison the man is acting very eager, rushing to pick up the tab, hovering at your chair to help you up and on with your coat, you might assume he's really keen and would like to see you again.

If the two of you allow a slight kiss, or a gentle peck on the cheek, this is also another good sign. But if the man stands in the door of the pub or café, his shoulders hunched, his chin low, eyes looking downward, it's safe to bet that he might want help in getting out of this situation without it appearing too awkward.

One or the other of you will have to raise the topic. Some people prefer to make the exercise academic, saying something along the lines of, 'Why don't we both go home and email each other with our thoughts or feedback?' That might mean he/she doesn't know what you think. Very often one or the other will come up with a line something like, 'I don't really think this is going to work between us, do you?' Also often two people agree half-heartedly to meet again, but then no one follows through. That's meant to be a gentle let-down, so no one has to really deal with the situation.

An off-hand 'Keep in touch, it was nice meeting you', can usually be read as 'Thanks, that was OK, but no more.' Another standard is, 'I've got your mobile number and email, I'll drop you a line soon.' That can be confusing if you don't hear from the person, especially if you'd really like to meet again or be given the chance to speak some more. All you can do is look reasonably enthusiastic and say, 'That would be really nice, I've enjoyed this evening.' Try to walk away with your head held high and not looking miserable. You don't want to be the hangdog, disappearing off into the night with your tail between your legs.

There's a lot of rejection inherent in the dating scenario. You just have to accept that is the name of the game. Ironically, some people feel rejected even when they didn't want to see the person again themselves. It's just that they'd rather be the one doing the rejecting, than end up as rejectee. So chin up, chest forward and onwards to the next date.

Follow-up

Can you follow up dates if they implied they'd like to meet again, but you haven't heard? Of course you can, but not tomorrow or the day after. Some people genuinely like to put a space of a week or two between dates, because they're busy at work, or following up other dates, or need time to take stock.

A man or woman is entitled to follow up if he or she was expecting a call or email, but don't let your expectations take you much further. If someone is not keen enough to be in touch again very quickly, then his or her interest in you might well be limited. He or she might be happy to get together for another casual date, or might be keen to have sex with you, but the silence is probably telling the tale that the person is not that keen for a full relationship, or does not want you to become deeply involved in his or her life.

However, that is also not always true, as we saw in the story of Jenni and Tom. Anything can have cropped up to take the person out of your sphere for a time. It's always worth giving someone a second chance, if you feel strongly enough about him or her. After all, your own level of interest and desire to see the person again might be the trigger that turns him or her around. Sometimes men and women are so unused to meeting a passionate response that they can be quite bowled over when they meet such a level of enthusiasm. Perseverance and trusting in your own feelings are valuable personality traits. Just make sure they don't slip over the edge into fantasy and obsession.

At least sometimes, you will make it to a second date. So let's move on in Chapter 6 to look at some of the valuable factors that will now begin to take on greater importance as the dating game hots up!

Chapter 6

Moving On Beyond the First Date

You met for a first date and something clicked between the two of you. Now you're about to meet for a second date. Either you made an arrangement to meet again during or at the end of the first date, or one of you has been bold and approached the other with a view to meeting again.

Please try not to jump ahead, so that you're ordering the wedding dress or holiday in the sun right now. Agreeing to meet for a second date in the normal world is fairly low-key on the commitment rating. Many people think 'Why not meet again?' even if they hadn't been struck blind by you, or vice versa, first time around. They might be meeting because there was a small inkling of interest, a tiny wee flame trying to get some oxygen to see if it catches fire. Or simply out of a feeling of friendship and 'no harm done', they think it'll be fine to get together for dinner, or whatever, if you were able to hold a decent conversation, had a few laughs and maybe even grazed each other's cheeks in tribute to the fact there is some warmth and the odd tingle there.

But ironically, such feelings can vanish altogether on the second date, when you're left exposed with your expectations and the odd inkling of 'Could this be the one?' OK, we all know that the correct advice is not to look at early dates with a view to 'Oh my God, could I marry this person? Could I live with him/her on a 24/7 basis?' But it is very hard not to do so. Even if you're thinking, I quite like him/her, and we could continue meeting on a 'friends' basis, the other person might not be reading the same message from the runes. Or the other person might be quite contentedly seeing you, making dates – but notably not at weekends, certainly not for Saturday nights – and you don't realise for some time that this is not going to develop into a proper relationship. For some people, that might be enough, and you could carry on for a long time without a problem, until perhaps one day something snaps and you begin to feel this is all one-sided, unfairly loaded in the other person's favour.

As we heard from Maggie in an earlier chapter, she was falling in love with Greg, who made it very clear that he was not going to single out any one woman for exclusive love and permanence, but she didn't listen to what he was saying. She continued to believe for several months that, surely if their passion for each other was sufficiently strong, he would change his mind. He never did shift his viewpoint. To this day, she is still in email contact with him and counts him as a true friend, but he continues on his chosen life-path.

Unfortunately for Maggie, she has met other men similarly unable to commit, and in time-honoured fashion, she continues not to listen or to deny what she is hearing. To her, as a more 'mature' woman, the dating pool can be treacherous waters. After months of rather disappointing meetings with men of her own age group, she was contacted by a good-looking, serious, rather shy and much younger man, 12 years her junior.

• • • • • • • • • • •

'I was just there for sex.'

Maggie: *He wanted me to come and visit him in his hometown on the south coast. He's very handsome and I found him interesting. He couldn't have been more keen to start with, and I saw in his attitude the possibility of a real relationship. The sex was fantastic! He seemed so keen on me. We were visiting and staying with each other once a fortnight, being very passionate, for about three months. Then I let out the fateful question. His birthday was coming up and I asked why I couldn't spend that weekend with him. He was very definite in his 'no', as he was going to be with family. So finally it was obvious to me, I was just there for sex and some companionship on the side. I'd never be brought into his circle of family or friends.*

He rang me a couple of days later to say he'd been pacing up and down the beach, worrying about it all, and we had to stop seeing each other. Oh dear, I'd staggered into a minefield of confused emotions there. I felt at the time it was the age gap, but it's more likely that he can't make relationships. He was late-40s, never been married, only once lived with a woman. Why did I go and misread the signals so badly again?

I can't blame online dating for that, as you could meet this kind of man anywhere. The good thing about being with him, though, was that I was now beginning to realise that I wasn't interested in guys my own age or older. So I found myself doing an internet search for sites where men and women of different ages could meet. www.AgeMatch.com is just that.

I was so nervous that I didn't put up my picture at first, but I was honest about my age and wrote something brief about myself. I couldn't believe it when several wrote to me immediately. Early on this really charming man who works in a City law firm wrote saying 'Could you cope with a 38-year-old?' He finally sent me his photo on email, and there he was looking gorgeous. We talked quite a lot and he was obviously very bright and clever. I couldn't understand why he wanted to be with an older woman. After several months of perfectly happy dating, and great sex, yet again I dared invite him to spend the weekend with me, or at least stay over a Friday night so that we could spend a more leisurely time in bed on Saturday morning. And that was it! He broke it all off.

• • • • • • • • • • •

Annie, in a similar age group, says:

> *I met a number of people and had a few brief relationships, but three months seems to be the crunch point. What happens is that you date a couple of times, then you enter sexual relations and it depends on whether you've already established a friendship or not. After a few weeks or months, it begins to fizzle out if one or the other of you realises this is not really 'the one'.*

When to arrange a second date

Of course it's a totally different story for those where the 'it' has happened and things are going to, or are likely to, progress. Where Sally and Jason (who we met earlier) were concerned, things had gone so well on the first date that he immediately asked to see her again and booked tickets for the rugby. For Maddy and James, things also moved smoothly. After their first date when they had stayed up talking till 5 am, this is what happened next.

• • • • • • • • • • •

'*We had a knee-trembling, melting kiss.*'

Maddy: *We knew we liked each other a lot. He phoned me the next day as he didn't want me to worry. I hate playing games and he sussed that. If you're interested say so. No rules, no games.*

We arranged to meet the following week, but now I'm getting a bit worried. I really like this guy and I don't want it to go too fast. There's another guy I'd had a couple of dates with and someone much younger and gorgeous was writing to me, so I decided to keep a few irons in the fire.

The second date, we had a good evening out and stayed chaste, with a nice little kiss at the end. The following Saturday, we met for birthday drinks of a friend. I got to meet his friends first, then we went to a party of my friends. I'm into techno music, it's not to everyone's taste, but he seemed to cope and enjoyed dancing. That night we had a knee-trembling, melting kiss and I ended up staying with him till Monday morning.

So there we were, it was all happening so quickly. I was desperately 'in lust' as well as enjoying his company. It just felt so right.

• • • • • • • • • • •

When is the right time to have sex?

What a loaded question. There are obviously no right or wrong answers here. If you're after lots of sex, without strings, there's plenty on offer out there, either through the internet or maybe from speed dating. But if you're looking for a proper relationship, it's likely that you'll wait at least till the third date before going full throttle with sex. For Mary Ann, who had now met her great big 6 ft 2 in (1.88 m) Sam, and who had been quite free sexually in her earlier years, things went surprisingly slowly:

We had a couple of dates and he was all gentlemanly, so much so that in the end I had to attack him at a bus stop. We finally kissed and I went back with him to his flat. My parents and grandmother must have been right all along, guys don't really want a long-term relationship with a girl they've shagged on the first date. And we girls like a bit of courtship too. He certainly doesn't know about my sexual past.

For Kathy and Mark, sex was certainly not top of the agenda, when they were seeing each other for those months she was still in Paris whilst he lived and worked in London:

Mark and I took six or seven dates before we even kissed and I wasn't certain in those early weeks how serious he was about me. Then it all happened very quickly. We were in love with each other and decided to move in together.

There does seem to be a consensus of opinion that if, as a woman, you want a good relationship, don't be too hasty to hop into bed. Let him get to know you. Both of you need time and space for some courtship, for romance to glow and for anticipation to work its wonders. No one wants to appear desperate or too needy.

On the other hand, there is also the view that you may as well get the first sexual experience out of the way, under the belt, sooner rather than later. If it is going to fail at the first hurdle and you are simply not turned on by each other, than it's maybe easier to back out of a would-be relationship in the early stages.

There are no hard-and-fast rules. You just have to take each person as they come and try to stick to your own beliefs and values. Certainly if anyone is trying to persuade you into sex, when you are unwilling (man or woman), do not give in to them. Query the person's motives. It's not only nervous young men who will try to beg women to have sex, implying that they are cold and frigid if they won't go along with them. It can happen at any age. Better that you build up your self-confidence and believe that the person is interested in you for yourself, rather than just for sex and some frantic attempt at intimacy.

Coping with nerves beyond the second date

Once upon a time, in the dim and distant past, a man would write love letters to a young woman. The letters would be delivered by a third party, she would read his words, be enraptured and eventually take up her quill pen to write back to him. The courtship would roll along nice and slowly until he eventually met with her father to propose marriage. We've all seen the Jane Austen films – or even read the books! But those days are so long gone, and we are in a completely different world.

Not that many years ago, courtship was often conducted by an intermediary, even if that person was your best friend, who would make the initial contact with a young man or woman and then report back on his or her feelings towards you. That best friend could also come in very useful if this young man or woman began to get a roving eye and started seeing someone else on the side.

But now, with the internet, email, mobile phones and text messaging, we none of us have any idea what the other person is really getting up to. Or, worse, if you are using an internet dating site and have met your new potential partner on that site, you might innocently go into the site again, only to see him in action with someone else. What do you do?

Welcome to life in the fishbowl! In a way, it should help us all feel some sympathy for celebrities, except their romances and love lives are acted out on the world's stage, with the media ever-present to report on the slightest slip-up or foible.

If you and your new partner are both members of an online dating site, until that time you both commit to the extent you agree to take your profiles down, freeze them, or at least hide them to concentrate on building up this relationship, you will have to live with the fact that you or your partner might still be flirting, chatting or even following up other leads.

What can you do about it? The best advice is to trust. Without trust no relationship can grow. With distrust, you will only back the other person into a corner and make him or her feel spied on, controlled, and even stalked. There are often genuine reasons for going back online, particularly if you feel part of a community. You might have built up friendships and want to continue emailing those new contacts. You might have new members making contact with you, and feel it's only polite to respond.

What you don't want is to be lambasted with emails from an aggrieved new date asking you why you're online when you are meant to be devoting your time to her or him. That, in all honesty, is a sure-fire way of bringing a fledgling romance to an abrupt end. So don't chase, pursue, hound or jump to conclusions. We live in this strange world of transparency, while at the same time the mobile phone is the one gadget that has given us all the ultimate opportunity to lie (or white lie).

It all comes back again to your level of self-confidence. As

Annie pointed out earlier, when you're talking to someone on an internet or chat site, you have to bear in mind he or she might be conversing, flirting, or arranging to meet with several other people at the same time. This is about that 'sweet shop effect' again. But, then, not everyone is so inclined, or so addicted as to not know when to stop. Let's return to Maddy's story one more time to find out how this great raging romance continued to roar its way into the blue yonder.

How to know if you're going too fast

You might find things really take off and all your friends and family are concerned, warning you not to go so fast. But then, again, what do they really know? Maybe it was meant to be this way. You read of all sorts of apparently 'instant' relationships taking place from couples who met online, or through introduction agencies. Just because endless Jeremiahs will say 'marry in haste, repent at leisure', sometimes destiny has come in to play you the best possible cards.

• • • • • • • • • •

'We came back engaged.'

Maddy: *Suddenly I knew I wanted to marry him. I said to myself, 'This man is going to be my husband.' What's weird is that I wasn't even that keen on the idea of marriage again. But one day, within those early weeks, I blurted out to him, 'Will you marry me?'*

We decided to go away together and found a cheap trip to Riga (Latvia) for our fourth week anniversary. I kind of knew he'd ask me to marry him when we got there – we both knew it. Riga was full of British stag-nighters, which can be quite a turn-off. But our time was all lovely and romantic. I'd brought my swish red dress and made myself turn out looking quite feminine for a change. He proposed and we went looking for an engagement ring.

We came back engaged, which freaked out everyone we knew. 'How can you possibly know?' they all asked. My parents only said, 'Are you really sure?' We decided that as we were going to live together, rather than one move into the other's flat, we'd find our own place and quickly get married. We were both so much enjoying the fun, romance and whirlwindiness of it all. We were rushing around meeting each other's parents, family and friends. His parents were of course also concerned.

We'd met in May, were engaged in June and got married on 9 September – and I wasn't even up the duff!

We moved into the new flat in north London in mid-July. Then it was wedding planning all the way. I wore a black corset with red dragons and a gunmetal skirt with sunflowers. He wore a grey jacket, black trousers and a dark red shirt. Our parents met the night before. No bridesmaids. The best man was his (female) friend. We wanted it to be just for us, not caring about conventions. We've even had our own crest created.

Maddy's verdict on those crazy few months:

> *It's back to ordinary married life and he still makes me ridiculously happy. We spend all our time making friends feel sick about us, we're so perfect. It's so strange that seven months ago I hadn't even met James, now I can't possibly imagine not being with him.*

• • • • • • • • • • •

For Kathy and Mark, things also progressed very quickly after a fairly slow and almost cautious start. Not having kissed for the first six or seven dates, as Kathy says:

> *Then it all happened very quickly. We were in love with each other and decided to move in together. We went travelling for six weeks to Japan and New Zealand. I guessed he'd propose to me, as we were going to climb a mountain, just before Valentine's Day, and he'd ascertained that it was the highest peak of our trip. But as it turns out that day was pouring with rain and we nearly got blown off the mountain. On Valentine's Day itself, I thought 'Sod it, I'll have to ask him.' I wrote him a haiku, and we got engaged on Valentine's in New Zealand.*
>
> *We were aiming to get married this November past, but having decided we'd start trying to get pregnant, it actually happened the very first month. The baby was due in December, so we put the wedding forward to April next. All this within the space of two years, and whoever would have thought we'd meet on an internet dating site?*

Are you moving too fast?

There are plenty of couples who do move too fast and live to rue the speed. You can probably only judge by your own gut reaction. Sometimes allowing things to move fast, throwing caution to the wind, brings out the best in us after years of non-committal, fear of rejection, worry and anxiety. But if you're feeling rather sad and lonely, you meet someone who comes across as far more stable, he or she courts you and you seem to slide easily to talk of living together and marriage, listen again to that gut feeling. Is the person maybe acting out of a disguised desperation and loneliness?

Annie talked of meeting a man through a chat room who proposed marriage to her within a week of meeting. The unfortunate truth was that he was a con-man who regularly fleeced women of their money. You will know, deep in your soul, whether the relationship is really worth pursuing. If in any doubt, give it some breathing space, back off and see what transpires. Likely as not, he'll move on to another unsuspecting victim.

There's one of those old proverbial phrases that your mother might say: 'If it's all too good to be true, it probably is.'

Listen to your gut instinct. If this person can only ever meet or talk to you at odd hours, and either doesn't want to or says he or she can't meet at weekends, the likelihood is the person is keeping from you a marriage, or maybe is living with someone, but enjoys love, sex or romance on the side. If the person can't be honest about that now, what hope is there for the future?

Although I advised you to steer clear of people who start looking you up on the internet, who try to trace where you live or your home phone number, it can be worthwhile for you to make sure you know something about the potential date before you agree to meet. Has he or she willingly given you his/her mobile phone number? Do you have his or her private email address? Do you know the person's surname, and has he or she told you something about his/her line of work, where he/she lives, and whether he/she has children living at home or not, for example?

How honest do you feel he or she is being? If people never answer your questions directly, but hedge around answers or return them with a question to you, they've maybe got something to hide. People can be private, but if you're looking to take this relationship further, you've a right to some basic information.

How often does the person phone you? Does he or she always call when he/she promises to, or do you get the feeling he or she is hiding behind text messages as a way of keeping you warm, without letting you get too close?

Even if the person won't let you meet any members of his/her family, can you be introduced to a friend? That's a good way to suss someone out more fully, to sec him or her in the light of one of his/her own friends. You'll maybe see a lighter more jokey side to him or her. Or will he or she agree to meet up with some of your friends, just for a casual social outing? If someone refuses all such suggestions, then you have to assume either he or she has something to hide, or he/she just wants to keep you in a little box, with the label 'sex, love or a bit of an adventure' on the side.

Be wary of declarations of love within a few days, hours or even under a week. Lust is different from real love. So is desperation. Be aware too that there are some really tricky characters who enjoy playing on people's emotions to take money from them. The perpetrators can be women as well as men.

Assuming all is going fine and you do progress to a normal relationship, like many of the stories we have been reading in this book, when it comes to the crunch and friends, family and colleagues want to meet your new partner, how brave and upfront will you be?

Telling people how you met

For all the brave talk, the success stories, the failures, the vision of the internet or other dating agencies bringing us closer together, has the stigma actually vanished from meeting the love of your life, or even someone with whom you have a relationship for a few weeks or months, by a method other than what is still seen as the 'normal' or organic way? The crunch might come when it means explaining to your parents, children, boss or colleagues how you and so-and-so met. Strangely, some of the boldest exponents of this form of introduction often react most sharply to the question, and men seem to be altogether more coy about divulging their hidden secret than many women.

Mary Ann, the young press officer in London, whose whole circle of friends use online dating sites, admits that when she was first using the internet as a student back in Australia about ten years ago:

I would never have told anyone that I met someone online. I'd lie and say that we met in a bar or through work or friends. I might not even now tell my parents. But among my circle of friends or work colleagues, I do believe the taboo has gone. We talk openly about it at work. Things have really changed so much. Sociologically, we can see how things have changed. I don't know anyone who met someone in a bar recently, got drunk and woke up with a complete stranger after having sex! Maybe by our age, late-20s to early-30s, we've moved on beyond that.

Of all people, Jez, who we met earlier in the book is one who stops short of telling his male friends how he has met his new female partners. He might sound very bold talking about his great sex life and how he finds it such a thrill to go out meeting new people, but when it comes to his mates at the running club:

I would never ever admit to them that I go into chat rooms and on internet sites. They'd think I was a real weirdo. I just tell them I've met a woman socially, if they get to meet. Women talk about sex and relationships to each other, but we guys don't.

However Jenni, who will emigrate to Australia with Tom later this year, says she is slightly more embarrassed than Tom to talk about how they met:

We went for drinks with a group of friends, including three other couples. Do you know, three out of the four couples met online. One couple is already married. There really is less stigma now,

> *particularly if you are living and working in a major city like London, where everyone knows the working hours might be 7 am – 9 pm. How on earth do you get to meet someone new, out of your friends' circle?*

So does the stigma still exist or not? Jenni also had this to say:

> *Neither Tom nor I really care, but I suppose some people do still think it means you're a sad loser. Last summer, we were at a music festival and I was all dressed up. Tom is cute-looking, but I must have come across as very glam. This guy stopped us and said to Tom, 'How did you get to be with her?' We both answered back instantaneously, 'online dating'. The guy shot back, 'Wow, what's the name of the site?!' It was a funny incident, but a bit demeaning all the same. Why did he think Tom was so lucky to pull me? Aren't I the lucky one too?*

For those of you brave enough to give the quizzes one last try, test yourself against this one.

Quiz

How do you know whether you've met 'The One'?

Most people who are happily settled will tell you that you 'just know'. For the rest of us, who haven't quite made it down the aisle just yet, we know that there is some kind of middle ground. Once you're settled down into wedded bliss, it can be hard to remember the early days of a relationship. You might be excited to see your boyfriend or girlfriend, and you have fun together. Everything may be looking rosy, but you haven't yet got that certainty that you'll be together for ever. This fun quiz will give you a helping hand to find out if he or she is really the one for you.

Make sure you answer the questions completely honestly if you really want to know the truth.

1. *If you haven't seen your boyfriend or girlfriend for a few days, how do you feel when you think about him/her?*
   a) Everything's fantastic and my life's wonderful now I've met the perfect man/woman.
   b) I smile. I'm so glad I met him/her.
   c) A bit nervous. I don't know what he/she's up to.
   d) Worried about why we haven't seen each other for so long.
   e) Mostly happy, but also worried about whether I'm doing the right thing.
   f) I don't know whether he/she's right for me.

2. *When you think about the future with your partner, are there doubts that sometimes spring to mind?*
   a) No. I know he/she's perfect for me.
   b) Not really. He/she occasionally makes me angry, but on the whole we resolve our differences well and we're really happy together. I'm fairly optimistic about the future.
   c) Yes. We can enjoy each other's company, but I sometimes wonder whether we want different things out of life.

d) I'm not sure if the timing is quite right for this to be a lifelong commitment.

e) Yes. There are positives, but I have major concerns.

3. *How many times a week do you spend time together as a couple?*

a) Every day.

b) Five or six times a week.

c) Three or four times a week.

d) Once or twice a week.

e) Less than every week.

4. *Imagine you introduced him/her to your parents (perhaps you have done already). How would it go?*

a) Really well. They'd probably think he/she was perfect.

b) My parents would be polite, but I'd be a bit embarrassed of him/her.

c) They wouldn't get on at all.

d) My parents wouldn't think he/she was good enough.

e) They'd get on well. Even if they didn't think he was completely perfect, they'd keep their views to themselves unless they had serious concerns.

5. *You're staying in for an evening with your boyfriend/girlfriend. The TV won't work. How would the conversation go?*

a) We'd have to go out for the evening instead.

b) We'd just have dinner, have a cuddle and go to bed. Probably not much conversation.

c) We'd stay up chatting for ages and have fun. We always have a lot to talk about.

d) We'd start chatting and probably end up bickering.

e) We wouldn't have much conversation. Our relationship is based on passion and we'd end up in bed before very long.

f) We'd probably have a romantic evening. We'd make dinner, have a long conversation, have a bath together and end up in bed.

6. *Could you imagine life without your partner?*

a) No. I think my life would be pretty empty without him/her.

b) It would be hard to imagine as I wouldn't want that, but I'm sure I'd manage.

c) I'd miss him/her, but I'd have quite a laugh being single again.

d) It's quite easy to imagine actually.

e) I couldn't imagine it as we're destined to be together.

7. *Would you stick by your boyfriend/girlfriend if he/she became unemployed and couldn't find a job a year later?*

a) Of course. Love is more important than money and status.

b) I'd struggle with it. There would be immense pressures, but I like to think we'd get through it.

c) I'd like to think we'd try but, realistically, I don't think there'd be much chance.

d) Truthfully, I can't see it lasting a year, whether he/she has a job or not.

e) Unfortunately not. I don't really want to date someone who's unemployed.

8. *You're going out for an evening with your boyfriend/girlfriend and a few of your friends. You don't really like his/her outfit – it's just naff. It doesn't look right and the colour doesn't suit him/her. What do you do?*

a) I'd have to say something. I couldn't let him/her go out like that.

b) I don't really like it when he/she wears things like that. I'm even a bit embarrassed.

c) I just think it's a shame he/she couldn't make more effort for me.

d) No one's perfect. I'm sure he/she doesn't approve of all my clothes either, but I'm not about to start asking for his/her approval either.

e) It's quite endearing really.

f) It just wouldn't happen. He/she has perfect taste. That's why he/she's going out with me!

9. *If you ever imagine spending the rest of your life with him/her, how does that make you feel?*

a) I'm not sure about it. I might feel differently in a year or two, but I can't help thinking I might miss out on meeting someone better.

b) I'm just not ready to make that sort of commitment yet.

c) I might feel happy about it one day, but not just yet.

d) I know we'll be together for ever and I'm happy about it.

e) We haven't really made that sort of commitment yet, but I'd be very happy if it ended up like that.

f) It makes me feel quite nervous.

g) It doesn't worry me too much. I just know it's not going to happen.

10. *Right now, if your boyfriend/girlfriend was offered a fantastic job in another area of the country, which meant he/she would be earning much more than you and he/she wanted you to move there too, what would you do?*

a) I'd ask him/her not to go.

b) I'd leave the decision to him/her, but if the decision wasn't staying here with me then I'd know the relationship didn't have a future.

c) I'd give him/her my blessing, but I wouldn't go too as I have my own life here.

d) We'd just try a long-distance relationship first and see how it went.

e) I wouldn't be thrilled at moving, but I'd probably go for it if he/she really wanted me to.

f) I'd jump at the chance.

11. *Do you feel that you get to spend quality time with your boyfriend/girlfriend every week?*

a) We see each other, but it's usually not quality time.

b) We try to, but our lives are so busy that it's often not quality time.

c) My partner's too busy to spend a lot of time with me.

d) My partner's not interested in doing the things that I want to do.

e) Yes, it's not always going out somewhere expensive, but we do have special time together at least every week.

f) Yes, we go on lots of exciting dates together.

Your answers

1.	a) 4	b) 3	c) 1	d) 2	e) 1	f) 0	
2.	a) 4	b) 3	c) 2	d) 1	e) 0		
3.	a) 4	b) 3	c) 3	d) 2	e) 0		
4.	a) 4	b) 0	c) 0	d) 0	e) 3		
5.	a) 0	b) 2	c) 3	d) 0	e) 2	f) 4	
6.	a) 1	b) 3	c) 1	d) 0	e) 4		
7.	a) 4	b) 3	c) 1	d) 0	e) 0		
8.	a) 0	b) 0	c) 1	d) 3	e) 4	f) 1	
9.	a) 1	b) 2	c) 2	d) 4	e) 3	f) 0	g) 0
10.	a) 1	b) 1	c) 0	d) 2	e) 3	f) 4	
11.	a) 0	b) 1	c) 0	d) 0	e) 3	f) 4	

Scoring

The answer's probably no (0–10)

What on earth are you doing with him/her? It seems you already knew the answer before you took the test. If it's just a casual fling, and your 'friend' feels the same, then it may be that there's no harm done. You just don't feel this is going anywhere, and most of us will have been here at some point. But proceed with caution. Sometimes it's just a stopgap, a bit of fun. Or it could be that you're playing games and not being honest with yourself or with your boyfriend or girlfriend. Or maybe it's a bad relationship that's gone on too long and it's hard for you to leave. Whatever the reason, you know your heart is not in it any more, if it ever was in the first place.

Might be potential but don't hold your breath! (11–26)
There could be potential here. It sounds like you have had some good times together, but you do have serious doubts. Our instincts tell us things for a reason. Perhaps you need to listen to what your instincts are telling you and why. Perhaps you're just in the very early stages of a relationship and you just don't quite know enough about the other person yet to know whether there's any future. But if things have been going on like this for quite a while, maybe you should ask yourself just what you want from a relationship and if it's realistic that you're ever going to get what you want here.

This could be the one (27–37)
You're not seeing things with rose-tinted spectacles, but that's no bad thing. There could be a fantastic future in this relationship if things continue to develop as they have done. If you have the odd argument, this certainly doesn't mean that the relationship is destined for failure. Healthy arguments are vital in a relationship. It's how you resolve matters when there's a

disagreement that's the important thing. It sounds like you get on really well with your boyfriend or girlfriend and you've grown really close. You can see he/she isn't perfect and you love him/her all the same. These are the cornerstones of a really healthy relationship. This one could really last the distance.

Rose-tinted spectacles (38–44)

Well, you've really fallen for him/her in a big way and your feelings are telling you that this is the one you've been waiting for. But just remember, seeing things as completely perfect doesn't mean things are that way in reality. In real life, no one's perfect, your boyfriend or girlfriend included. You may well have a very happy future together, but bear in mind that at some point, you're going to find out that there are things you disagree about and there will be habits that you find irritating. Burying your head in the sand and becoming over-sentimental about the relationship and the future is not going to do you any favours in the long run. That said, we all tend to lose our heads a bit when we fall in love. It just might be that you lose your head a bit more than most.

Chapter 7

The Business of Love

Some sceptical people question whether the fact that online dating sites, introduction agencies, and even those involved in putting on social events to bring singles together, all create a healthy income for the entrepreneurs behind them, means that their value is tainted. In my opinion such a view is outdated, and harks back to the stigma that used to be involved in the dating game. Those of a certain age might remember that any singles outfit was tarnished with the brush of the 'lonely hearts' tag, and the assumption that such people were sad losers who obviously parted with their money far too easily. Now that we live in a more sophisticated society, and singledom is a necessary part of most adults' lives at some point, I do hope we've moved on, beyond the stigma.

There are some very good people out there helping to sustain the interface between services that the internet (and phone, email, texting, etc) can bring us, so that you and millions more men and women can have a good chance of meeting some new potential partners, hooking up for casual sex, or perchance, meeting that someone special who will be the love of their lives.

There is also a large pot of gold under that same rainbow and plenty of keen entrepreneurs are keen to grab some of the stash. But then the internet has created a whole new breed of (sometimes) exceedingly rich new businessmen and women in a variety of areas.

Going back to the statistics, they can truly shock us with their awesome size, as the internet dating market has shot up to stardom in the past five to six years. The UK dating market now turns over some £60–70 million (forecast for 2007). In the United States the figure is a staggering $1 billion. However, the trend is not all upwards forever and evermore. Once a large proportion of adult men and women have signed up online, or started speed dating, the problem for entrepreneurs can be in keeping the upward growth. Where the UK market is still growing exponentially, the US market for example has recently seen a slowing down in market growth (following a surge of 77 per cent in 2003), and in 2006 it was only growing at 7 per cent a year.

The initial upsurge of online dating has been from the young, free and single, as is also truc of speed dating and other singles social events. But that is now changing. The new driving force in terms of growth in both markets is coming from the age 50-plus market, as more men and women who are getting divorced find themselves single again and refuse to believe that's the end of a love life for them. One in five marriages ends in divorce, with the famous seven-year itch still holding true (the average time of marriage before divorce is seven years and three months). In this country alone there are about 155,000 divorces granted every year, most ending because one or both partners no longer feel compatible and want to experience the heady heights of being in love again.

Which online dating sites should you trust?

Interestingly, the first people to sign up to internet dating sites in the United Kingdom came from the more serious, professional middle classes. Why? Not because there were more singles in that sector, but because computer use even five to ten years ago was found in the more highly educated professional group. Computer usage and the subsequent fascination and trust in the internet began in academia. By now it has spread to all areas of society. I'm going to profile some of these more serious sites, as they have given time to helping me research this book.

The *Guardian* newspaper's Soulmates (www.guardiansoulmates.com) site was launched in 2004–05. The newspaper decided to grow an already successful printed personals advertisement section onto the web in a very bold move. The *Guardian* was taking an active interest in the growing popularity and widespread use of the internet in all its forms. It had the data to start up from those people who were already advertising on the personals pages. After extensive market research it set about creating a user-friendly site, which was advertised through the newspaper. It then discovered that men and women were really keen to sign up. Being able to post up your photo, scan and read profiles, and be matched against a selection of criteria (eight or nine in this case) seemed very attractive. In the early days, more men than women would sign up, a reflection of the fact men probably felt more comfortable with the internet in those days and, perhaps too, less squeamish about putting their personal details up in a public domain.

The choice of name for the website was important. The name Soulmates didn't sound like some free sex site, and it also helped create the feeling that *Guardian* readers could create their own small 'club', or 'social network'. The membership database continues to be relatively small, compared with some of the major players in the market, with active membership at about 40,000 subscribers. The paper made a deliberate decision to go it alone and keep its own database discrete, thus helping members feel that they are part of a small club of like-minded people. *Guardian* Soulmates works in partnership with Telecom Express, which provides the back-end technological support, and the income is shared.

By contrast, the global site PlentyofFish was founded in 2003 by Markus Frind as a way for him to practice his ASP.net programming skills. The growth since then has been driven by word of mouth referrals. PlentyofFish now gets 400,000 user logins a day and Markus continues to operate it himself from his Vancouver apartment, and has declined numerous offers of venture capital funding. The average age of the American PlentyofFish members is 39. PlentyofFish is the most popular dating site in Canada, the 6th most popular in both the US and the UK.

Another British site, www.loveandfriends.co.uk, grew from the already established personal introduction agency Drawing Down the Moon, and in 1999, was one of the first to launch in the country. At the time, online dating was seen to be very much an American experience. The agency decided to grow the internet site out of its current membership, as many potential subscribers to the agency either could not afford the relatively high fees, fell outside the prescribed age range, or lived too far from London and the south-east. It also decided to pitch the site away from the big, aggressive mostly US sites, giving it a more homely face and targeting directly graduate professionals.

Loveandfriends still sees itself as quite small, with an active membership of about 110,000. It was launched with free membership for everyone registering in the first year. As there were only limited numbers of members on the Drawing Down the Moon database, the site also advertised in the national press and *Time Out* magazine. The first year was a real challenge, but now it is well established and finds that up to 75 per cent of new members come from having been recommended by a friend who has recently found a new partner. A successful site comes down to the quality of its members and the numbers, in all age groups and across the nation. Keeping up the new member subscriptions can be tough going. The need for new blood has been described as a beast that has to be fed every month: one with an insatiable appetite.

Whereas the site was set up more or less by one man, a computer and a book on how to create a website at his side, it now employs eight staff to work the customer service side. Like the other respectable online sites, all profiles are vetted, photos are looked at carefully, credit cards are matched to the person's name and IP address. Staff answer queries and complaints or, more happily, congratulatory letters and emails.

The site www.parship.co.uk was launched in the United Kingdom relatively late in 2005, from its German base and pan-European membership. Across Europe it has over 2 million members, with some 140,000 in this country. It rates as a relatively expensive site as it offers an 80-plus item questionnaire and takes security very seriously. Parship won't accept any customer without checking the profile, photo, IP address and credit card details, to make sure that it all matches up.

The photo is often the first giveaway. Fraudsters might use stock model shots or scan in a magazine photo. The personal profile copy is read and approved before it goes live. Time-wasters are weeded out by a reasonably high monthly charge, and that members have to devote time to filling out the personality questionnaire and writing a decent profile. If you've gone through those hurdles, it should be clear you're serious about finding a relationship.

Free dating sites

So is there a real problem with the free dating sites? Remember the saying about there's no such thing as a 'free lunch'? Well, the same holds true for 'free' commercial TV companies, and similarly 'free' dating sites. The payment comes in your exposure to advertising, marketing and sales.

Free dating sites are not really offering much of a service, other than coming up with a huge database of people, which you can then browse or search. They need a critical mass of a list of names (and emails) of 500,000–1 million people, which they sell on to large companies that are also eager to market, such as Tesco. They make their money from advertising and links to other services.

One of the problems with the free sites is that people can pretend to be more or less whoever they want to be. You can lie about yourself, or just completely oversell yourself. PlentyofFish was set up specifically to be free, and maintains this viability. It matches on the basis of behaviour. Realising that people essentially exaggerate in their profile answers, the owner and founder decided that actions essentially speak louder than words. For example, if a woman says in her profile that she is looking for a solid, stable man who earns $100,000-plus, but she keeps clicking on profiles of muscle-bound bad boys, PlentyofFish makes sure she meets plenty of under-employed weightlifters, and some of the stable ones whom she tends to ignore. People don't even realise the site does this. They just see they are getting results. This strategy is akin to grocery store purchase tracking.

PlentyofFish also claims to be high on the marriage stakes. One weekend, the site launched a section devoted to member marriage stories. Within three hours, 90 marriage success stories had been uploaded, and five days later there were a total of 295 marriage stories, complete with photos.

Trading personal data

If you sign up to one of the free sites, you might suddenly find you're being bombarded with junk mail, spam and maybe computer viruses. No doubt we should all be reading the small print on any site we sign up to, but that doesn't seem very romantic, does it? However you might well have signed your agreement that the owners of the site can sell, trade and distribute your data to whomsoever they want. Indeed, your email address can be as much of an asset to that kind of site as your premium membership fee is to the paid-for site. The email addresses are traded for profit: hence the need to have as large a database as possible.

Google searches

Market position and getting your site's name known, talked about and a good reputation is vital in any e-business. With so many sites available (just look at the amazing list in the Resources section), they are obviously in deep competition with each other. The really big sites that have a global reach such as www.match.com and in the UK www.DatingDirect.co.uk can plough millions into huge television advertising campaigns or outdoor posters. They also pay PR companies or do work in-house to promote themselves as widely as possible. Most newspapers now have an online dating section, which has grown up with the classified advertising pages – you hunt for the love of your life alongside the second-hand cars.

The link with the personal ads in print newspapers is still very important, as those ads lead to people paying for voicemail messages that other users then phone into and pay for again. So the income from the telephony side of this market continues to be vital. Newspapers are actively working to integrate the personals ads into their online dating offering. If you place a personal ad, you will now also more than likely have an online profile. But the personal ad is completely out in the public domain, so your information can be accessed without anyone having to pay upfront. This gives you maximum coverage. Your voice message can be accessed online or through the paper, and responses can be made either online or by phone. The online sites have overtaken the personals ads, but newspapers are reluctant to let go of the visible print classified ads that have been a major hook for readers for many years.

Most of the advertising spend for all online sites, however, is on keyword activity with Google. Even the smaller sites have to invest in 'affiliate marketing', whereby affiliate management specialists farm their banner adverts out to the zillions of websites on the internet. And all the companies pay small fortunes to Google each month. Loveandfriends, for example, claims it is spending £10,000 a month for 'click' marketing, which means it is paying for sponsored links, and bidding for available words such as 'single' or 'dating' to get high up the Google search. In such a competitive market, there is an element that the big guys are forcing the smaller operations out as they force up the costs. All anyone can say right now is that the market is new, competitive and constantly evolving. So watch this space!

In the meantime, just like any other corporate raiders, the major players in the field are eyeing up new markets. China has become the latest target. The big timers such as eHarmony and Match.com are hoping to link with Chinese partners to promote internet dating services in 'an effort to explore new profit streams in emerging markets'. Sources predict that the Chinese market could grow by some 60 per cent to produce annual revenue of nearly $85 million in 2008.

The same faces on different sites

It is true that many men and women post themselves up on one or two (or even more) dating sites, using different user names, to give their profile more of a fighting chance. You might recognise some of the same old faces. Generally speaking, that is not a case of fraud or anything untoward, more the inner determination of this person to get out there meeting lots of new people.

Behind the scenes, however, there is one other marketing ploy you should be aware of. Many of the bigger sites provide a 'white label' service for other clients. For example, I explained that the *Guardian* Soulmates site is given its technological back-end and support by Telecom Express. That company is also providing back-end services to *The Times* newspaper's online site, to *The Scotsman, Daily Telegraph, Observer* and *Financial Times.* DatingDirect provides its white-label service to high-profile respected brands in the United Kingdom such as AOL, Channel4.com, HeartFM.co.uk, iVillage.co.uk, NTL and Tiscali, to 'name but a few' as they explain on their site.

Parship.co.uk provides a similar white-label service to many of the leading media outlets such as *Hello!* magazine, Independent newspapers, Express newspapers and *Metro,* the free newspaper.

Truth and untruth

Is the object of your affection for real? Honesty, schmonesty – there's lying, white lying and just a little deception. Or there's major fraud and scamming. The Russian brides scam is the kind of story that does the rounds from time to time, and when you start to look into it it proves very interesting.

There is a small industry out there, along with the letter from a distressed gentleman in Nigeria asking you to invest millions in his unknown company, that plays on people's needs and desires. The person posing as a beautiful young Russian woman seeking love with a western man may be living in Russia, or he/she may be anywhere in the world. The profile is made up, the photo is usually of someone stunningly pretty, and behind the scenes is an email targeting job either virally eating into the internet and ending up in random inboxes (including my own sometimes), or attacking the online dating sites posing as a proper member.

When a man writes back, the fraudsters start an email correspondence. They might even speak on the phone – the scammer will have a woman on hand to talk nicely by phone if necessary. In a couple of months, it's agreed that the woman will come over for a visit. She claims she'll buy her own ticket, but then there are last-minute visa problems and she won't be able to come if she can't produce a large amount of money at the last minute. He sends the cash by Western Union – and that's the end of the story.

However, the story is not so cut and dried. There are genuine Russian women seeking partners in the United Kingdom or United States. There are plenty of men who want to meet them, and so now there is another counter-business offering advice and help on how to ensure the sites or agencies you use are scam-proof.

But scams, con-men (and women) and fraudsters have always been part of our lives. If you are genuinely interested in seeking a relationship with a Russian woman, or with someone from another country such as Thailand, the Philippines or China, then it's worthwhile doing as much research as possible into finding safe sites and advice.

Preventing the scammers

As I explained earlier in this chapter, if you sign up to a reputable paid-for online site then it will be on its guard against fraudsters. After all, the sites don't want a bad reputation as that would destroy their image. Bogus profiles are taken down. Sham photos are examined. The industry needs its good professional image.

One of the many new companies being set up to counter all the attacks that are made on the internet includes the US-based HonestyOnline. It offers a certification system that takes the 'lie out of online'.

'It's an extra layer of protection to determine if a guy is Jack the Ripper with three wives,' said William Bollinger, executive vice-president of National Background Data, LLC, which invented CrimSAFE, a database used by HonestyOnline. Along with the background checks, HonestyOnline can show up at your house, snap some profile pictures, stand you on the scale, run a tape measure from head to toe, and even, if requested, leave with bodily fluids to assure potential mates you have nothing communicable. After you pass muster, you graduate to a sticker on your online profile testifying that you are ready for love.

Services which allow users to cross-reference members across social networks and dating sites are beginning to emerge in the United States. Some services such as www.freckl.com show the newest members on a collection of dating sites and allow you to bookmark and tag their profiles. Others allow users to see what other people think of an individual who is a member of several dating sites.

For example, US-based MateCheck's new technology 'connects' these accounts and creates a profile, including real name, phone number, and AIM screen name:

> *Since its launch in 2005, www.MateCheck.com has collected comprehensive reviews and character ratings for over one million men registered with such sites as Match.com, EHarmony, Yahoo Personals and JDate.com. 30 million women have visited an online dating site seeking a lifelong partner without knowing that 30 per cent of men registered on these sites are already married or living with someone. MateCheck's exclusive DateScore technology determines a man's authenticity based on objective information provided by women with first-hand knowledge – the women who have already dated him. No longer is she dependent on his self-evaluation as described in an online dating profile. Using www.MateCheck.com, women can view an unbiased report as to who he undoubtedly is, and what he's really about.*

Nobody has yet set up a tailored version of this idea for UK daters. There is a feeling here that personal safety is the responsibility of the individual, and we would not be so keen to have the big brother element, or nanny state, attempting to curb our fancies or fantasies. Background checks can be unreliable and cumbersome, and might rather tarnish the appeal of the potential knight in white armour. Keep your wits about you and stick to basic personal safety and security habits. Then there should be no more problem with getting to know someone through an online dating site than if you met him or her on the street or in the pub.

Conclusion

A final word

The bottom line is that anyone is lucky to fall in love, to meet the man or woman of their dreams, and for that relationship not only to spark, but catch fire and continue to smoulder. We should all feel immensely grateful that love does happen, and that in a cynical and over-exposed world, the simplest of emotions – love, trust, sexual attraction, companionship, compatibility and support – survive and are distinct possibilities for most of us.

So if you are out on the dating scene, please don't feel embarrassed or that there is any stigma attached. Feel proud and confident that you will meet someone one day soon. In the meantime, try to make the most out of your dating adventure. I wish you all the very best of luck in your searches.

Resources

Online dating sites: UK and Europe (or global)

www.guardiansoulmates.com
www.parship.co.uk
www.loveandfriends.co.uk
www.eharmony.com
www.match.com
www.DatingDirect.com
www.meetic.co.uk
www.lovecontacts.uk.com
www.quickflirt.com
www.canoodle.me.uk
www.Date.co.uk.
www.plentyoffish.com
www.midsummerseve.com
www.girlsdateforfree.com
www.loopylove.com
www.udate.com
www.okcupid.com
www.wheresmydate.com
www.isawyouonce.com
www.datemyplate.com
www.darwindating.com
www.mysinglefriend.com
www.TypeTango.com
www.JungDate.com
www.Pocado.com
www.Interrodate.com
www.ivorytowers.net
www.Easyrencontre.com
www.CapFriends.fr
www.2Become1-fr.com

Married but looking for other relationships

www.illicitEncounters.com
www.lovinglinks.co.uk
www.passion.com
www.lonelycheatingwives.com

Older men/young women; older women/young men

www.sugardaddie.com
www.agematch.com
www.toyboydating.com
www.YouCanGetMe.com
www.gocougar.com

Friends . . .

www.friendfinder.com
www.makefriendsonline.com
www.friendsreuniteddating.co.uk
www.newfriends4u.com

Single parents

www.kno.org.uk (Kids No Object)
www.datingforparents.com

Over-50s

www.FiftyAlready.com
www.laterlife.com

Religion or ethnic based

www.relationships.com
www.bigchurch.com
www.jdate.com
www.ukafro.com
www.arabium.com
www.WhichOption.com/dating
www.singlemuslim.co.uk
www.asians4asians.com
www.email4loveasia.com
www.shaadi.com
www.JapanCupid.com
www.Love21CN.com (China)
www.ChineseLoveLinks.com

Gay dating

www.gaydar.co.uk
www.nerve.com
www.planetout.com

Introduction agencies (on and offline)

www.drawingdownthemoon.co.uk
www.sara-eden.co.uk
www.seventy-thirty.com
www.execclub.net
www.thecountyregister.com
www.berkeley-international.com
www.grayandfarrar.com
www.meetyourfuture.co.uk
www.destinajapan.co.uk
www.attractivepartners.co.uk
www.onlylunch.co.uk
www.justwoodlandfriends.com

Websites for singles events: UK

www.thesinglesolution.co.uk
www.meetatlast.com
www.execeventsclub.co.uk
www.thesinglescalendar.co.uk
www.single-london.com
www.uksinglesnight.co.uk
www.club-class.co.uk
www.ukevents.net
www.urbansocial.com
www.iVillage.co.uk
www.gradulicious.com
www.cosmoparty.com
www.xfactordates.com
www.chemistryevent.co.uk
www.dancedating.uk.com
www.strictlydancingpartners.co.uk
www.kcdating.com
www.dinnerdates.com
www.speedbreaks.co.uk
www.speeddatinglondon.co.uk
www.speeddateronline.co.uk
www.onlylunch.co.uk
www.nexus-uk.co.uk
www.saga.co.uk/sagazone

Community 'social networking' sites

www.myspace.com
www.bebo.com
www.urban75.com
www.secondlife.com
www.facebook.com
www.linkedin.com
www.friendster.com
www.friendsreunited.co.uk

US dating sites

www.Yahoo Personals.com
www.Singlesnet.com
www.eHarmony.com
www.Mate1.com
www.AmericanSingles.com
www.TRUE.com
www.Gay.com
www.eCrush.com
www.chemistry.com
www.MatchDoctor.com
www.VietSingle.com
www.BookofMatches.com
www.SparkNetworks.com
www.Singlesnet.com
www.BlackPeopleMeet.com

Australian dating sites

www.singleswhoclick.com.au
www.ezifriends.com.au
www.rsvp.com.au
www.soulmades.com.au
www.matchfinder.com.au
www.theloveclub.com.au
www.companions.com.au
www.singleconnexions.com.au
www.cupid.com.au

Reading matter

Ben-Ze'ev, Aaron (2004) *Love Online: Emotions on the Internet*, Cambridge University Press, Cambridge

Appendix

The language of online or text dating

If you're new to chatting and messaging online, you might be a bit bamboozled by the strange symbols and acronyms that you see cropping up in chat, message boards, emails and Instant Messages. Fear not – these are simply abbreviations designed to save the typist time and make the best use of their limited screen space. They can also give a greater degree of personal expression to online conversations. Here's some advice courtesy of www.AOL.com/dating.

There are certain basic principles and rules observed by this type of chat language. Certain words may be represented by a collection of letters and/or numbers that sound the same when said aloud but which take up less space (eg m8 = mate). Smileys, also known as emoticons, can be used to represent a facial expression and add emphasis to a comment (eg :-) is a smile).

Other tips to remember include marking 'actions' between either < >, * * or :: :: symbols. For instance, if you want to show someone affection, you could type <hug> or <kiss> – to which the other person might respond with a <blush> or <g> (grin).

Then there's typing in capitals. Although you might type a word in capitals for emphasis, to the online world, typing entirely in upper case is construed as SHOUTING and might make people <frown> at you.

This guide to the most popular symbols and phrases should see you through your cyber-conversations. It should also provide you with inspiration for your own abbreviations and smileys – these expressions can also be a lot of fun for users to devise and share. As well as being very easy to use, this cyber-shorthand is also respectable enough to have been recognised recently by the *Concise Oxford Dictionary*, which now includes several of these phrases!

You can also add more character to your online presence with AOL's 'My Expressions'. You can choose a cool Buddy Icon from its colourful selection, pick out your own set of smileys and choose yourself a complete desktop theme. For more information about these options, visit AOL Keyword: Expressions.

:-) Ch@ing (happy chatting)!

Smileys

When you are chatting in chat rooms or via IM, the person or people you are chatting with can't see the expression on your face or hear your tone of voice. Therefore, they could misinterpret what you are saying. Using smileys (or emoticons) at the end of a sentence can remedy this. A smiley face or a wink can let people know you mean your comment light-heartedly or tongue in cheek, and you can even use a smiley to give someone a virtual hug or kiss.

Here is just a small selection of the many possible smileys available. There are lots of variations, and it can be fun to make up your own to trade with people you meet online.

General smileys

:) or :-) or :o) Smile

:D Smile/ laughing/big grin

:(or :-(or :o(Sad face/frown

:| Grim face

:* or :-)x(-: Kiss

;) Wink

:X My lips are sealed

:P Sticking out tongue

{} A hug

{{{{{{{ }}}}}}} Lots of hugs

:'(Crying

O:) Angel

':) Raising one eyebrow

,:) Raising other eyebrow

8^[Stuck up/fed up

}:> Devil

>:-{ Hurt and angry

:-` Hint of a smile

:-@ Not feeling too great

:-! Used unrepeatable language

<——— Referring to yourself

$) I love money

:-& Tongue-tied

<|:-) Witch

":¢(Punk smiley

Acronyms

If you want to send someone a quick message that gets straight to the point, you may not have time to type out a full sentence and punctuate perfectly. But quite literally at your fingertips are countless time- and space-saving acronyms that will instantly get your meaning across. They will not only help you to get your comments in quickly to a fast-moving chat room, but also lend an air of friendly informality to your conversations.

As with smileys, other members are always inventing their own expressions, but our guide to the most commonly used should get you started. The most popular are listed below, but read our expanded guide to acronyms for a more extensive list.

General acronyms

<G> Grinning
A/S/L Age/Sex/Location
AISI As I See It
B4 Before
B4N/BFN Bye For Now
BRB Be Right Back
CIO Check It Out
CSL Can't Stop Laughing
CUL8R/CYL See You Later
F2F Face-to-Face
GR8 Great
GTG Got To Go
HAK Hugs And Kisses
HB Hurry Back
IDK I Don't Know
IDTS I Don't Think So
IMO In My Opinion
IOW In Other Words
IYKWIM If You Know What I Mean
IYSS If You Say So
J/K Just Kidding
KWIM Know What I Mean
L8R Later
LMK Let Me Know
LOL Laughing Out Loud
OIC Oh, I See
OMG Oh My Gosh
OTOH On the Other Hand
PLS Please
ROTFL or ROFL or ROTF Rolling On The Floor Laughing
SWDYT So What Do You Think?
THX or TX or THKS Thanks
TYVM Thank You Very Much
WB Welcome Back
WDYS What Did You Say?
WDYT What Do You Think?
YGBK You Gotta Be Kidding

About the Author

Carol Dix is an established journalist and author. She started her career by joining the *Guardian* newspaper as a young graduate and then moved into freelance writing for major London newspapers and magazines, before uprooting to New York for ten years where she continued to ply her trade in journalism and books. On returning to London, she turned to corporate writing, editing and producing in-house magazines. For several years she was head of communications for a university in London and has since gone back to her preferred 'portfolio' career, mixing consultancy in communications, media and PR, with feature writing and books, along with some teaching in journalism. The online environment has long been an asset to her, for work and socialising. Have computer, will travel . . . .

Other books by Carol include: *A Chance For The Top*, *The Camargue*, *D H Lawrence and Women*, *Enterprising Women*, *Her Royal Destiny*, *The New Mother Syndrome*, *Pregnancy*, *Preventing Miscarriage*, *Say I'm Sorry To Mother* and *Working Mothers*.

I'd Rather be Single than Settle

Satisfied Solitude and How to Achieve It

Emily Dubberley

From our childhood we're fed stories of finding our Prince Charming and living happily ever after with 'The One'. But is being attached really all it's cracked up to be and do we need an 'other half' to be complete?

In *I'd Rather be Single than Settle*, Emily Dubberley upturns the media stereotypes of desperate singletons and blissful couples and explores the real world of the single woman. Celebrating the best things about independence – the close friendships and great nights out, the chance to further your career and follow your dreams – she also gives practical advice on overcoming the downsides. Find out how to deal with smug couples and meddlesome mothers who can't accept your solo status, as well as how to beat the blues when the loneliness kicks in.

Packed with case studies from other spirited singles, *I'd Rather be Single than Settle* is the essential guide to singledom. After all, life's too short to settle!

Non-fiction: Self-help/Relationships

1-904132-98-7

UK: £10.99

US: $17.95

www.fusionpress.co.uk

The Ex Factor

Relationship Baggage and How to Deal With It

Emily Dubberley

In any relationship, there's one thing you're almost guaranteed to have in common with your partner: exes. In this insightful guidebook, Emily Dubberley identifies all the major issues that can crop up with both your and your partner's exes: jealousy, insecurity and one-upmanship.

Is it acceptable to ask a partner to get rid of all souvenirs of previous relationships? Should you try to stay friends with an ex, and, if you do, how do you handle it when they start a new relationship? Should you admit to how many exes you've got or blur the figures to sound 'better'? And is there ever any good reason to ask your new partner: 'Am I better than she was?'

Find out what the way your partner treats his exes says for the future of your relationship and learn all the essentials of *ex-iquette*. If you've ever dated before, and plan to again, you need this book.

Non-fiction: Self-help/Relationships
978-1-905745-17-3
UK: £10.99
US: $17.95
www.fusionpress.co.uk